A Soul Reclaimed

A Soul Reclaimed

A Young Woman's Escape From Sexual Slavery and Servitude

(A true story; only the names have been changed)

Lou Guzzo

Writers Club Press
San Jose New York Lincoln Shanghai

A Soul Reclaimed
A Young Woman's Escape From Sexual Slavery and Servitude

Writers Club Press
an imprint of iUniverse.com, Inc.

For information address:
iUniverse.com, Inc.
5220 S 16th, Ste. 200
Lincoln, NE 68512
www.iuniverse.com

ISBN: 0-595-15354-2

Printed in the United States of America

To all the Grandmas of the world who instill faith, love, and a penchant for beauty in the hearts and minds of their grandchildren without seeking a reward...

And to all women still awaiting freedom from the brutal treatment of men who persist in the medieval notion that women must serve them, no matter what the cost in body, mind, and spirit...

And, finally, to the enlightenment of all those men who have not yet learned that the tradition of subjecting women to daily servitude belongs to the past and to history.

PREFACE

In more than a half century of service as a reporter, newspaper editor, TV commentator, and author, I have been privileged to meet and know intimately a most remarkable cast of unforgettable characters. Some of them were condemned to lives of pain, brutality, and severe mental anguish. Some were schemers or thieves. And some were saintly in their service to others. And still others were heroes and heroines. But none that I have known created a deeper impression on me than a young woman named Sarah, about whom this book is written. I could not use her real name, because her life remains in danger, despite the fact that she has overcome monstrous obstacles to regain her soul. The tragedy is that there remain throughout the world many, many more Sarahs, who may never have an opportunity to follow her example and reclaim their lives and their souls.

—Lou Guzzo

CHAPTER I

On the morning of her 40th birthday, Sarah Dawn Summers looked hard and long into the mirror on her dresser, as she had done so many days of her life.

She knew that the image she saw was much too slim for her five feet eight inches of height, but that could be fixed. After all, hadn't her nose been fixed? Remember that godawful schnozzola she'd been born with and the terrible pain she had gone through to carve it down to reasonable size? How could she forget it? And the coarse, black hair that looked more like a discarded hairbrush? Thank God she had taken the frizzle out of it at about the same time a surgeon gave her a new nose in her late teens and handed her a new life, as well.

The onetime ugly duckling was now a reasonably attractive, somewhat svelte woman of the world. She liked everything she saw in the mirror—except those eyes! The millions of tears that tried to find their way out but never made it in a lifetime of abuse, violence, and sexual harassment had left their mark nevertheless. They were tired eyes, sad eyes that seemed to be saying, "Please listen to my story before your eyes grow like mine."

Sarah sat down in the dresser chair and let her mind wander....wander back to her childhood. If *it* had not happened to her, she would have been a nonbeliever. And if *it* had not happened to

her at about the age of 6, she wouldn't be alive this day and recall-
ing her past before the revealing mirror.

She pointed a finger at herself and saw the finger point back at
her. Furthermore, she reminded herself, if *it* had not happened to
her, she would not have survived the ten years of hell she lived
through as a young woman, a decade of decadence in which her
soul was, in effect, for sale to the devil himself.

The vicious, constant beatings administered by a drunken father
first brought *it* on. When her small, bruised, and abused body
finally could absorb no more, she simply removed herself from that
body in protest against the pain. That was *it*. Ridiculous? Of course
not. Out-of-body escapes from pain have been experienced by
thousands, perhaps millions, of others, some of whom have been
courageous enough to chronicle their stories of abuse.

Sarah knew she owed her gratitude to all those brave people in
all corners of the world for daring to reveal their out-of-body experiences. They had made it possible for her to tell her story to friends
and therapists without concern for those who might question its
credibility. All she could do was tell it as it was and hope that in the
telling she might save other women from experiencing the tragedy
in her life.

She waved her finger at herself in the mirror and nodded her
head slowly as she reminded herself that her story should be specially important to men, mainly to those who believe they must
resort to brute force and inhumane treatment to control the women
in their lives.

Firmly chiseled in her mind like a message on a gravestone
was a headline she had just read in the newspaper: *"Why men
kill women they love."* The article, written by a *New York Times*
reporter, recounted the brutal deaths of two young women and
the near-death of a third, all in different areas and circumstances. In each case, they had been attacked by men with whom

they had been living and loving for some time. And, strangely enough, all three killers committed suicide shortly thereafter. Was it delayed justice?

The reporter's words seared Sarah's memory and sent a chill down her spine as she remembered how many times the elders in her family had reminded her that a woman's primary role in life was to please her man:

"According to statistics collected by the Federal Bureau of Investigation," the reporter wrote, "32 percent of the 3,419 women murdered in the United States in 1998, the latest year for which data are available, died at the hands of a husband, a former husband, a boyfriend, or a former boyfriend." However, the article went on to say that, because of the limitations of the FBI's data-gathering methods, the true figure was much higher—perhaps as high as 50 to 70 percent!

Psychiatrists and scholars were asked why men are so much more likely to murder their partners than women. All of them responded that such crimes reflected a society in which men "feel entitled to exercise power and control over women and to use physical violence when necessary to assert their dominance."

Sarah shuddered as the memories of her own life jolted her into grimacing at the image in the mirror. She remembered that the incessant, alcohol-driven abuse in her life began very early in her childhood in the small Canadian town of Lethbridge, Alberta, 80 miles or so north of the U.S. border. She was the oldest of four children, and because of that, more was expected of her than of the others. That's why she had to take the blame and the beatings for whatever went wrong. She wasn't the only one to suffer. Her mother took many of the beatings, too. Mom had not laid a hand on Sarah herself, undoubtedly because she, too, was the victim of her husband's drunken wrath and found no pleasure in resorting to violence herself.

Dad would beat Sarah fiercely for little or no reason at least two or three times a week. Sometimes more. It was a blessing that he was gone much of the time as a traveling salesman of vacuum cleaners, cars, and whatever else grabbed his fancy. Had he not been on the road so much, it is probable that neither Sarah nor her mother would be among the living today.

One incident she remembered above all others. A friend of her father's had been visiting and they spent most of the night drinking themselves into a stupor. Mom came home from her evening job to face a husband who was rip-roaring drunk, as usual. Although Sarah should have been sleeping by then, she heard Mom come in and jumped out of bed to go down the hall to greet her. She tiptoed past the bedrooms of her sisters, Elaine and Marian, and her brother Steve, and went quietly toward the living room. When she heard her father yelling furiously at her mother for a reason she didn't understand, Sarah froze and peeked around the corner into the kitchen, where they stood. A moment later he picked up a coffee pot from the stove and hurled it at Mom, who was standing only a few feet away. It struck her flush in the face and she fell over backward, screaming.

Sarah wanted to scream, too, but no sound would come out. After a moment of paralysis and horror, she crept back to her room, fearful that if she were detected, she would get the same treatment. Mom, stoic as always, insists she doesn't remember the incident. But Sarah knew it was simply her own way of defending against pain; by denying it, she could pretend it never happened. The time would come when she would face reality and take action to save herself—and Sarah—from destruction.

The family's life in Lethbridge was cast in the shadows of poverty and chronic despair, urged on by family traits that went back at least three or four generations. Alcohol and violence were the family fuel. Little wonder that breaking the law seemed to accompany those characteristics. Back in the Great Depression years, one member of the family kept dodging the law in two countries with illegal sales of liquor across the American border and an elaborate scheme for dodging police on both sides of the border. Like an old movie about bootleggers and rum-runners, he and his cohorts had arranged for a series of warehouses with trick floors and doors that helped hide his contraband trucks from highway patrols that picked up his trail. He never spent a day in prison, mainly because he found a few key "friends" in customs on both sides of the border.

The irony of it was that the bootlegging relative was one of the few in the family who treated Sarah with kindness. Although he has long since gone to his reward, she was grateful that he gave up his illegal practices and tried to reform, but it didn't take. He died of alcoholism.

The strains of alcoholism and violence seemed to be congenital in the family.

The suspicion certainly was there. Maybe science will provide the world some day with the information needed to change the course of human lives devastated by such maladies. In the meantime, Sarah would continue worrying about it. She also wondered what kept her from being like her hard-drinking Great-Grandma, a dark legend in the family, who was not only an alcoholic but extremely cruel as well.

Stories about her were passed along in the family and related her special cruelty toward her own children in the harsh winters of Montana. Not only did she "cat around," as members of the family described her sexual indiscretions. Her discipline of choice toward an errant child was to put him or her out in the snowbanks for the slightest misbehavior. And the enforced punishment lasted for hours. Her children soon learned, as they had to, that they could survive by finding or digging holes underneath the house to take whatever cover and warmth they could manage. Her "sentences" to the misbehaving children included threats to kill them if they didn't mend their ways!

One of the reasons for her incredible actions was the fact that, with her husband gone on the road so often, she often entertained gentlemen friends, and she did not want any children in the house at the time.

Sarah ruminated about why someone didn't tell the police about her brutality toward her own children. It must have been, thought Sarah, that in the earlier part of the century, "child abuse" was accepted as the "norm" and the prevailing logic was that "children were to be seen and not heard." Also unheard of then was the term, "sexual harassment" of women—a term underlying Sarah's own story that emanated from the family background of cruel behavior, excesses in the use of alcohol and drugs, and the debasement of women.

It seemed impossible for such a succession of corrupt characters to emerge from a frontier environment like Western Canada's, but Sarah had seen firsthand that it did. The miscreants in her family line, however, were the exception, not the rule, but they were a powerful exception that cast an enormous shadow over the rest. Among the rest were a few "good folks," who disdained or eventually gave up heavy use of alcohol, free sex, and violence, or at least made an attempt to do so. The bootlegging relative who tried to reform was one.

As she continued staring into the mirror, Sarah lost track of time and consciousness, as her early years unfolded before her, like an old movie. Despite the bitterness of her childhood, she remembered some of the happy times that made the bitter ones all the more painful.

There she was, dancing, running, and even giggling as she played games with her brother and sisters in the large house alongside the prairie. She recalled frequent references to her as a "big" child. It seemed everyone commented she was truly an adult in a child's body, and she didn't understand why it was said. Her senses were stimulated by the memory of fresh prairie air, the sweet smell of the large pine tree in the spacious yard, and the sweet smell of the raspberry bushes that seemed to protect the dark, moist ground.

The huge apple tree in the middle of the yard was the perfect setting for what should have been a continously happy childhood. More than the apples, the tree provided welcome shade in the hot, prairie temperature, particularly when the Canadian chinooks exaggerated the heat from the boiling sun. Even Swarn, the friendly neighbor from India whose last name she never knew, would leave his home nearby to come sit with Sarah and the family under the apple tree. All of them enjoyed a cold glass of grape Kool-Aid, Sarah's favorite.

On days when the sun was gone and snow drifts were everywhere, Sarah and her brother and sisters spent hours playing in the basement. They would play hide-and-seek, and Sarah boasted that she could never be found. A large, old bed dominated the expansive basement, and all four youngsters pranced upon it as if it were a circus trampoline—until the day the springs, mattress, and wheels gave way, almost in relief. A game of tag was made risky because it was done around the old oil furnace. Whoever made the painful mistake of slipping and suffering a burn on the hot metal surface was, of course, out of the game.

Daredevil Sarah smiled as she saw herself, at age 7, sneaking out of her bedroom window, which permitted an opening of only a foot. It was a tight squeeze, but it made the adventure all the more worth while. She couldn't remember why it was so important to escape from the second-floor window, but she recalled a sense of freedom on the outside. Afterward she would run around the block in rapture as the cold wind whipped her hair. Her adrenaline rose and she "felt alive." Part of the rapture was in smelling all the flowers—the huge, pink peonies, lilacs, and roses, and making dancing ladies with hollyhocks. Those times, so short-lived and in such great contrast to the more frequent miserable times, were special to her. Where, she pondered, did they go?

Sarah realized she had always had a super-active imagination. Because of the trauma of her early years, she often thought that her only escape route was death itself. She tried learning to breathe without having her chest rise or fall, just as she believed she could become invisible by refusing to talk. Little wonder that she developed the automatic habit of turning herself off with the approach of pain.

The Summers house, which Sarah acknowledged was never truly a home, was always full of cats, because both Mom and Dad loved them. Sarah, on the other hand, took a great liking to mice; it could easily be construed to mean she learned to love mice as a rebellion toward her cat-loving parents. At any rate, Sarah continued the love affair with mice until the night she took her favorite pet, a while mouse she had named Chi Chi, to bed with her. Chi Chi's greatest achievement was that she hopped, instead of walked.

When Sarah awoke in the morning, she found Chi Chi under her, "flatter than a pancake." She cried uncontrollably as she placed the animal in a box and buried her in the backyard. Sarah was inconsolable. How could she hurt a creature so frail and gentle as little Chi Chi, whom she had grown to love with all her heart? In later years, she found the situation one of strange comfort. She alone knew the pain she felt for the small creature of God. Much later in life, however, she realized the false premise she had adopted. If no one knew her pain, they could not know the real Sarah.

Despite the interludes of normalcy and childhood happiness, Sarah recognized that her early life was a living nightmare. But what, she ruminated, did a child know until he or she relives a past that is full of destructive adult relationships? Her parents were married young and both had come from extremely battered families. Theorists believe abuse is passed on from one generation to another, and Sarah's story was no different.

Her mother was young and active, and she loved life. Sarah believed that in the beginning of her mother's marriage, she loved her Dad. But when the drinking became excessive, the physical and mental abuse took form and became a reality for Mom and all the children to witness. That was when Mom's love turned to disdain and, eventually, hatred.

As it always did, the mirror image gave way to the most notable and lovable relative in Sarah's life, her Grandma Summers. With apologies to her own Mom, Sarah realized that Grandma Summers **was** her mother. Mom was seldom available to the children. Because her husband was away so much and contributed little to the family, she had to keep a full-time job that took her away from the household from 5 each evening to the early morning hours. She would be up in the morning to prepare breakfast and send the four children off to school, but they saw little of her most of those early years. That's one of the reasons Sarah had to assume many responsibilities with her younger sisters and brother. And it's also the reason she was given the blame and the beatings when things went wrong. Elaine, Marian, and Steve were much too afraid to own up to misbehaving, so Sarah would have to take the licking. After all, she was in charge, wasn't she?

Grandma Summers was a very different story. She not only had time for Sarah. She made time for her. In her early years Sarah often considered suicide to find relief from the abuse, the beatings, the boredom, and the violence. If it hadn't been for the kindness of Grandma Summers, she might have put an end to it all.

Grandma Summers was a kind, loving, caring woman, with a very large body and heart to match. She stood 5 feet 11 inches tall. Born in Devonshire, England, she had a gentleness and generosity Sarah admitted she had not found in any other human being.

She didn't have a mean streak in her, which made her so very much unlike her son, Sarah's father. Why, then, did he not inherit her kindness and goodness? The answer lay in the torture she herself went through at the hands of a maniacal husband, Sarah's grandfather, whose cruelty toward his wife included repeatedly stabbing her! When she was eight-and-a-half-months pregnant, Grandpa Summers confessed he wanted to cut the fetus from her body. One of the stories Sarah had heard but refused to believe was that Grandpa Summers had once chased his wife around the barn and the farm one day, knife in hand. But he didn't make good on his intention for reasons the family never understood. He was one of the few males in the family—perhaps the only one—who disdained alcohol, so he had no excuse for his strange behavior. Sarah's father had some model!

Grandma Summers had started life as a Mormon, because that's what her parents were, back in England. Then she tried Scientology, Christian Science, Evangelism, and several other denominations, most of them in Canada, never settling on one. She tried them all. Despite her religious shopping, she never faltered in her faith in God. Sarah was sure God understood the shopping.

Furthermore, Grandma Summers, more than any other person, instilled in Sarah the religious faith the young girl had not found in any other members of the family. Despite her own tragedy, Grandma insisted on putting the family above all other considerations and that it was most important to maintain a strong faith in God. That's where her strength came from. It was a lesson she passed on to Sarah and a lesson that probably saved her life.

Whenever Sarah went to visit her, which was often, she'd always coax her to pray along with her. She would say:

"Sarah Dawn, you need to pray to God. God is your savior and God will take care of you."

They would kneel at her bed and pray. There they were, Great Big Grandma and Little Sarah Dawn reciting the Lord's Prayer and other prayers she taught the child. It would have made a great Norman Rockwell magazine cover. They did that every day Sarah visited, which soon became every day of the week. Grandma also taught her the value of "nice things," as she put it—lovely pictures, vases, simple furnishings, beautiful people. Nothing ornate. Nothing grandiose or expensive. Just the things that made Sarah smile without being funny. Most of all, she taught the young girl the value of a frequent hug and kind word.

Grandma Summers also taught Sarah the importance of making people comfortable, making them feel worthy, and making them feel special because they were God's children. She showed Sarah how to make little ballroom dancers out of hollyhock blooms.

A broad smile lit up Sarah's face as she probed deeply into the mirror and said to herself, as if she were afraid of forgetting:

"Thank you, Grandma, for teaching me things I never learned anywhere else. Whenever I think about you, and that's often, I think about lilacs, African Violets, and hollyhocks."

She blew a kiss into the mirror.

Grandma created a safe environment for Sarah to dwell in, a beautiful island away from the turmoil she had known all her young life. If only it could have continued.

The most amazing factor of all was that Grandma Summers was legally blind! She had lost 90 percent of her sight to cataracts when Sarah was about 5, but it never deterred her. Her early adherence to the questionable precepts of some of the religions she tried on for size had caused her to be wary of doctors. That may have cost

Grandma her sight, but it didn't damage her faith. Despite her blindness, she moved around briskly.

Sarah was amazed by the ease with which Grandma found her way to Sarah's house and then back to her own, all without a cane or other help. She knew exactly where to go and never fell nor was injured.

It was God guiding her, she said, and Sarah believed it, then and now. What impressed the girl most of all was that no one ever heard her complain about her blindness. To her, it was a blessing, not a misfortune. Sarah would go to her house every day after school, and they would always have high tea, complete with the customary breads, cookies, and cheese. Veddy English, of course. And what did they talk about? Sarah couldn't remember! And why should she? They talked of everything and nothing at all. They just talked. In her presence Sarah felt ten feet tall and walked on air. For her, Grandma's home was an oasis of beauty, a Paradise, an escape from the ugliness she had come to know too well. No beatings there. Not even a single unkind word spoken in anger.

Grandma had a large porch that was typical of so many homes then. The porch was filled with African Violets, "thousands of them," as Sarah remembered saying at the time. Of course, there were probably about ten or a dozen, but in her young mind's eye they looked like "thousands." Grandma also kept her clothes closets out there on the porch, because she liked her clothes to be crisp and cool. Naturally, she wore the rayon floral dresses that were so very English. The house was always immaculate, unlike Sarah's, and everything had its place. There was no clutter, again unlike home.

On Sarah's seventh birthday, Grandma Summers brought a seven-layer cake to the house for the birthday party. Each layer was a different color and each had a different frosting. She had so many ways of showing her love. Sarah never knew how she got that enormous cake from her house to Sarah's without help. But she didn't have to know.

When Sarah left Lethbridge at 11, Grandma Summers had just been diagnosed with bone cancer. Saying goodbye was doubly painful, because she thought she might never see Grandma again.

She did see her once more, but it was a day her heart broke. It came when she went with her mother to Alberta to visit Grandma on her deathbed. Great Big Grandma Summers had been worn down to 80 pounds, and Little Sarah Dawn was once again praying with her at her bedside—for the last time.

She tried crying, but the tears, like the screams of other times, would not come. Grandma Summers has been gone for many years, but Sarah still kneels at her bedside every evening and offers a special prayer of thanks to her for saving her life and teaching her the real meaning of goodness. The pity of it is, Sarah thought, that there is so little of it.

CHAPTER 2

Sarah's departure from Lethbridge had a bittersweet flavor that never left her memory. It was November 9th, a very special day, because it was Grandma Summers' birthday, the only birthday celebration that excited the little girl, except for her own birthday, of course.

At the age of 11, she wasn't yet fully aware of the seriousness of Grandma's illness, so she looked forward eagerly to visiting her and offering her the small gift she had wrapped herself with lots of love. To her, Grandma's birthday was an event that transcended Christmas itself. But it wasn't to be.

"I'd like you to wait a moment before you go to school," Mom said without explaining.

"But, Mom, I have to go and see Grandma. She's expecting me before I go to school. And it's her birthday."

Mom was firm. "You can see her later. I want you to stay home for a while."

She told Sarah to go out and play for a few minutes, and she did. The wind had come up and a snow flurry descended as if on command, which was no surprise in the Canadian prairie. Sarah began making pathways in the snow, as she had done so many times before, and she was so busy that her suspicions weren't aroused when Mom sent Steve and Elaine off to school without her. Marian was still at home.

Minutes later Mom appeared at the door.

"Come in and put on your new red coat and boots and mittens. We're going out and I want you to be warm."

Unquestioning, Sarah ran in to get her coat, boots, and mittens and presented herself to Mom in the kitchen. There were two large suitcases on the floor and atop them were two or three heavy blankets. Mom had little Marian in hand.

"Hurry! We have to run. And don't ask any questions. At least not now."

They left the house and made their way through an alley to the home of one of Mom's best friends, Ann Johnson. All the way there, Mom lugged those two heavy suitcases and blankets with strength the children didn't know she had. Sarah had put her favorite pet mouse under her coat collar, but Mom didn't seem to mind. She had other more important things to think about at the time.

After ten minutes of furtive conversation, Ann and Mom led Marian and Sarah to Ann's car. They drove off to the home of a man Sarah had never seen nor known.

He was in a hurry, too. "We have to get going if we're going to make the bus." That was all he said.

The bus? What bus? Sarah's mind somersaulted. Now, suddenly, an incident involving her father began to make sense. One night he had come home, drunk as usual, and ordered Elaine to go and play in another room with Steve and Marian. He took Sarah to her bedroom and sat her down on her bunk.

In retrospect, she didn't know why they had the terribly bright lights in the room, but he turned them on full force and approached her. It was like a third degree. From that time on she hated and avoided bright lights. The blinding lights and her father's voice seemed interrelated.

"Sarah Dawn, you've gotta make a decision. Right now! Do you want to stay with me or go with your mother?"

Sarah said nothing, because she didn't know what to say. It should have been obvious to him that she preferred her mother, but if she said so, she'd be inviting another severe beating—which she got anyway. For what seemed like hours, she tried to hide under the blankets, sobbing but again without tears, as he continued to badger her, repeating the question in 20 different ways: "You have to make a decision, your mother or me?"

It was the first indication she had that a split was in the works. On several other occasions, he would awaken her abruptly from a deep sleep to repeat the question and threaten more beatings. Terrified, she learned to sleep lightly and always expect the worst.

She once had a recurring dream of her father beckoning her to go with him to her bedroom when no one else was in the house. Under the threat of another beating, he forced himself upon her and she shrieked with pain before blacking out and retreating once more into her out-of-body world. Was it a dream? Perhaps. Therapists have tried to coax more details from her, but that was as far as her dream would take her. Like so many ugly details of her early life, it lies buried in the darkness of a scarred young mind.

Sarah would never understand why her mother endured his beatings, heavy drinking, and carousing with women for so many years without rebelling. She knew he was seeing another woman, a woman he eventually married, but for years she pretended nothing was wrong and insisted that it was a woman's place to accept her lot, take the beatings and abuse, and not complain. After all, wasn't that the order of things? But even her long-suffering mother finally reached a boiling point.

The anxious voice of the driver jolted Sarah's deep thought. "Please, I said we have to get a move on if we're gonna make that bus! Now, come on!"

He had an old Barracuda parked in his driveway, and the three of them were stuffed into the back seat, like olives in a bottle. Then Mom, Marian, and Sarah were covered with blankets and their ride began.

Sarah still couldn't understand why they had to travel under the blankets. The trip seemed a lot longer than it was, because her troubled mind was thinking a million thoughts, all of them bad. Not a single word was spoken the entire time. She knew Mom would not harm them, so she wasn't worried on that score, but the flight under blankets was truly scary for children of 11 and 5.

At Coutts, Alberta, the town at the border crossing, they were rushed from the car and marshaled into a waiting bus. Still no explanations. Nothing. Sarah couldn't remember the brief conversation with a customs officer, so complete was her bewilderment. The bus took them to Shelby, Montana, and there they waited to board a train for Havre, Montana.

Sarah was beginning to feel like a character in a great movie chase, but she didn't know who was chasing them, why they were doing so, and where they were headed. She had plenty of time to let her mind wander, because it was a terribly long four-hour wait in the Shelby train station.

They were hungry, tired, and confused. Mom took the girls to the ladies' room and told them to stay there.

"You stand by the door, Sarah Dawn. And if you see your father coming, you run and tell me."

It was the first admission from her that they were running away from father and that he might be on their trail in his car. Knowing now who might be chasing them didn't soothe Sarah, because she knew what brutal beatings were in store for all of them if he found them and took them back home to Lethbridge.

Finally, the train for Havre arrived. The ride there was uneventful, again marked by an eerie silence. At Havre, their first chore was to find a hotel, because it was late and they had to spend the night there. Directly across the street from the station was a ratty hotel, like the kind seen often in Western movies. They didn't have much choice, so Mom asked for a room and immediately put Marian and Sarah to bed. They couldn't help but notice that as Mom undressed for bed, a number of greenbacks fluttered out to the floor as she took off her bra and girdle.

Sarah hadn't said much till then. "Mom, can you tell us what's wrong? Where are we going and why are we going? Please, Mom...."

Throughout the entire episode, Mom remained calm, as usual. It seemed that nothing could ever disturb this rock of Gibraltar. Sarah was sure she inherited that trait from her, but were reticence, silence, and Gibraltarism the way to go in a family crisis?

"Nothing's wrong, Sarah Dawn. Just go to sleep. Everything is OK."

The thought skipped through Sarah's mind, as it would many times thereafter: How much better off would Mom and all the children have been if she had stood her ground years earlier, faced her drunken, violent husband, and tossed a few threats of her own at him? It's the question Sarah insists is the impetus behind her need to tell her story.

"I'm leaving your father." There. Mom said it, without fanfare, without remorse. She didn't go into a long explanation of all the reasons for her action, but the children didn't need a dictionary of abuses now that the line had been drawn at last.

"Why are we going away with just Marian and me? What about Steve and Elaine?"

In a very quiet and subdued voice, Mom answered: "Well, I just thought Steve would be better off with his father. And your father always liked Elaine best of all. So..." She let her voice trail off, as if she were thinking about what might have been in a calmer, more orderly family.

"I wanted you with me, Sarah Dawn, because you don't get along with him. And you can take care of Marian." End of explanation. No tears. No anguish. No breast-beating.

Sarah couldn't help feeling sorry for her, even though she was comforted by the thought of being free from the monster who had beaten her so hard and so often in her young life that she had to escape to an out-of-body existence to relieve the pain.

That's all the conversation the forlorn threesome had that evening. The next morning they went back to the train station, where Mom bought tickets. On a wall was a large map. She pointed to Minnesota.

"There next to Minneapolis is St. Paul. That's where we're going to live."

Sarah burst out crying. "Mom, I want to go home and I want to see Grandma!"

Mom slapped her face and suddenly seemed more surprised and mortified than Sarah was.

"You have to grow up! You will not cry! You must not cry! You are now an adult!"

It was the first and only time her mother had struck her, and Sarah was certain Mom immediately felt worse than she did. The slap was a slight tap compared to all those her father had administered. But the shock to both of them was instant.

Mom has no recollection of that slap. Denial, again. But Sarah would never forget it. Mom realized that the usually reliable and responsible Sarah Dawn had lost control and cried in desperation. And calm, equally abused Mom couldn't handle it. That's why she slapped Sarah.

Sarah was sure she could never, ever imagine leaving two of her children. But Mom had made a decision, such as it was, and Sarah somehow got in the way of that decision there in the Havre train station. Young Sarah came to realize it very well may have been the

best and most important decision Mom ever made to escape from
the brutality, the slavery, and the ignominy of an impossible marriage. She remembered the stories her mother and other family
members had told about the once-great love story that had brought
her father and mother together.

Her father was Kenneth Orrin Summers, a traveling salesman
who sold vacuum cleaners and cars and whatever else he could
latch onto—when he wasn't drowning in booze and the pleasures
of forbidden women, that is. His mother and her family were
Mormon, but he didn't practice what they preached, particularly
when it came to absorbing alcohol, a no-no in the Mormon book.
He was a very handsome man, who resembled Burt Reynolds, the
movie heartthrob. When this Lothario of the Road came into
Mom's life on a visit to Havre, he bowled her over. She didn't buy
a vacuum cleaner from him, but she bought his line and the Burt
Reynolds profile.

They were married when he was 23 and she 19, and he took her
to his home town of Lethbridge to live. That's where Sarah was
born just 11 months later.

The family once referred to her as a love child, a cruelly ironic
label. What Mom didn't know at the time, because she was deeply
in love with her traveling Don Juan, was that he was having an
affair with another woman at least two months before Sarah was
born. In that first year of marriage, Mom now admits ruefully, he
was generous and kind and attentive—the few times he returned
home, that is, from his adventures in sales. What changed him into
the monstrously cruel husband and father he soon became?
Probably a combination of alcohol, womanizing, machismo, and,
what Sarah believes was most important, his inadequacy as a
provider and particularly his own childhood experiences of abuse.

After Sarah, in short order, came Steve, Elaine, and Marian. All
but Marian, Dad's "little baby," absorbed his continuing violence

and abuse, along with Mom. Undoubtedly, little Marian escaped because she was too young.

The pattern of alcoholism, violence, and abuse ran through Sarah's family on both sides, with a few exceptions. Because Mom had a difficult time making ends meet, she had to go to work as a waitress to keep the children in three squares all those years. That's why the children saw so little of her at home—and the reason Sarah became so reliant on Grandma Summers. It also meant Sarah had to grow up far too fast, so fast that she hardly remembers having the kind of childhood most others talk about. She was a surrogate mother.

The beatings administered by her father were usually applied with a razor strop. It was never a pat on the butt. Instead, it was drop your drawers and whop! whop! whop!, often until blood was drawn or the screams became deafening, even to him.

To this day, the sight of a razor strop causes her to panic and breathe hard, even if she sees it in a catalogue. The threat of punishment was painful by itself. She can remember the time when she was about 5 that her mother set up her ironing board in the living room. The iron was on the board and very hot. Dad walked by and said in that stentorian tone of his, "Don't touch the iron!" It was as if he were daring one of the children to touch it.

Like the rebellious child she was, Sarah naturally had to touch the iron. Wouldn't other precocious kids do the same? The pain was like a dagger to the heart, and she ran off to the bathroom to soak the blistered finger in cold water. But she made not a single sound. She didn't dare, because she knew the razor strop would make the pulsating finger seem to be mild pain by comparison.

Her father loved cars and, most of all, he loved to drive like a maniac, especially when he was in one of his drunken stupors, which was often. On Sundays—the Sundays he was at home, that is—he would pile all the children into his car, with Baby Marian at his side, and he would take off like a race-car driver. Mom always worked Sundays, so she wasn't there to curb his escapades. Not that she could have.

The wild rides would start in mid-afternoon, by which time he had already consumed a half bottle or more of rye. First he would take the children to the local A&W and order rootbeers for all four. Then he would head for the giant earth mounds everybody called coulees that dotted the prairie alongside the river. The mounds ranged up to 500 feet high and were blown smooth over the years. With drunken relish, Dad would drive over them at high speeds, paying no attention to the children's screams as they bobbed up and down hysterically.

Sarah wondered how they lived through those rides, although, once again, her fear would cause her sense of feeling to desert her body, as usually happened when the threat of pain approached. The more they cried out for him to stop, the faster he would go and the more he would double back over those mounds. It seemed that their agony only goaded him onward.

As a child, Sarah was prone to car sickness. That added to her misfortune, because when she would get sick in his car on those terrifying rides, he would beat her even harder with his razor strop. The smell of regurgitated rootbeer is hard to take, even for an adult who has rendered himself senseless on a bottle of rye. Forever after, Sarah would become ill immediately at the smell of rootbeer.

Dad had a sweet tooth. With Mom gone so much, he would make fudge or some other kind of dessert, including cakes, for himself and for the children. Sometimes there was hell to pay, because Elaine and Steve, who were always getting into something mischievously, would get into the frosting before he applied it to the cake. No one ate anything or tasted anything before Dad was ready to eat! Even if the children were hungry, they couldn't eat a thing until he gave the word. When he found out that someone had been into the cake frosting, he lined the four offspring in front of the living-room sofa and barked:

"All right, who did it?"

Elaine, Steve, and Marian immediately began to bawl. Sarah refused to cry. Even substitute Moms don't cry. When Dad repeated his demand for a confession and added, "OK, you're all going to get a spanking if you don't tell me who did it," the wailing trio went up an octave.

In desperation, Sarah would say, "I did it!", even though she hadn't. Of course, it meant another session with the razor strop, but she couldn't stand hearing the kids cry. After all, she reasoned, she was really their Mom and she had to take care of them. They got used to the idea and let Sarah take the rap for all of their misbehaviors.

How she spoiled them! She blamed herself. If she had forced them to own up to their misdeeds, they would have been better served later in life. And so would she.

Mom suffered his beatings in silence. Perhaps she did so with the knowledge that he would soon be out on the road again and absent for many weeks. What may have been the last straw for her and the incident that probably persuaded her to free herself at last came on their last Thanksgiving Day (Canadian Thanksgiving, that is) in Lethbridge. Mom had spent hours preparing a beautiful holiday dinner and had invited her mother, Uncle Roy and his two sons and their girlfriends, and several other people. The time came for all to be seated for the feast.

Dad, red-nosed from an all-day drunk, sat down to carve the turkey. After tasting it, he exploded, got up from his chair, picked up the turkey from the platter, and hurled it through the dining-room window, the glass splintering everywhere, like bomb fragments. Then he stalked off, complaining loudly that the bird had not been cooked enough. No one dared speak for at least four or five minutes. Needless to say, there wasn't much to be thankful for that day. Sarah ran off to her room to avoid the embarrassment Mom had to endure.

There was little worth remembering about those early years in Lethbridge. The family lived a hand-to-mouth existence, because neither Mom nor Dad brought home enough income to relieve their dreary existence. Theirs was a life of near-poverty.

Sarah doesn't recall many happy times, and most of them came when she was able to steal away and enjoy the warmth and love of her gentle Grandma Summers. The family didn't celebrate holidays. With Mom and Dad always in a combative state and with his incessant drinking and wielding of the razor strop, what was there to celebrate?

The holidays that appeared on the calendar were treated like any other day, including religious holidays. Neither Mom nor Dad belonged to any church and neither acknowledged a religious belief at the time. Sarah would have followed their lead if it hadn't been for Grandma Summers, who not only showed her the beauty and need of a strong faith but demonstrated it in all her actions and her affection for Sarah.

Holidays? No one was willing to risk another debacle like that miserable Thanksgiving Day. Everyone concerned, particularly Mom, was truly thankful—thankful that it would not be repeated.

Sarah didn't have a pleasant memory of Lethbridge itself, which is all prairie adjacent to the Canadian Rockies. Thanks to her early years in that environment, she couldn't tolerate heavy winds. It had something to do with her distaste for the dust, dirt, and debris the severe winds brought from the Rockies to the Alberta prairie. It also helps explain why she couldn't stand to have her hands dirty. Dirty hands are reminders of a painful, bitter childhood.

She often wondered what that childhood, and, indeed, her life, would have been like if she had had a kind, loving father, instead of a violent tyrant. She had to amend that. Dad did have something he loved dearly. It was his pet cat, Satin, gray with a white-diamond shape on her chest. In fact, he loved cats, all cats.

In the Summers' backyard were a large apple tree and a cluster of raspberry bushes. Sarah would crawl into the bushes, because they made an excellent hiding place. Armed with rhubarb from the garden and berries from the bushes, she would dunk them in a sugar jar she'd pilfered from the kitchen. One day she had retreated to her improvised den in the bushes and was dunking rhubarb and berries while seated like Pooh Bear. A weird smell interrupted her little feast. She searched the bushes and, to her horror, saw Satin lying dead. Someone apparently had poisoned her. Sarah never went back into those bushes again.

Fortunately, she wasn't blamed for Satin's demise. But more disturbing to her than anything else was the fact that her father was devastated by the death of his pet. From his bereaved reaction, she realized he loved the cat more than his children.

CHAPTER 3

The mind is a camera that collects the pictures the eyes snap throughout life, managing to save a precious few of them for instant recollection. For Sarah, one of the photos that remained framed in her mind was the scene that anxious day in Montana.

She will never forget the picture of Mom standing in front of the huge map in the Havre station. Trying not to show her irritation and worry, she had pointed to St. Paul as their destination as if she were playing a game of pin the donkey. Why had she chosen St. Paul? Because, she said, it was one of the places her husband was least likely to search for them in order to haul them back to Lethbridge. And, besides, she added in what sounded suspiciously like an afterthought, old family friends she might call on in an emergency lived in Chicago and could get to St. Paul in a matter of a few hours. Remembering the picture in the train station, Sarah has always believed Mom's choice of St. Paul was as accidental as pinning the donkey. But the stakes were considerably higher than those in a child's party game.

The train ride from Havre was a nightmare. Why it took two full days and two nights Sarah never knew, but it seemed even longer than that because she was sick the entire time—vomiting frequently day and night. Motion sickness again. It was a reminder of the wild rides Dad subjected her to on the prairie coulees of

Lethbridge. The horrible train ride would have been much worse had it not been for a black porter (she never learned his name), a very kind man in his early 50s, who befriended Mom and tried everything he could think of to soothe Sarah's heaving stomach—in vain.

When they arrived in St. Paul, she was a basket case. The porter helped them off the train and into the station.

"My girlfriend, Gloria, works in the women's lounge," he said to Mom. "Just go in there and get your daughter comfortable. Then we'll see what we can do to help you."

Gloria was as helpful and kind as the porter had been. She took Sarah into the women's lounge and pointed to a cot. What a blessed relief! Lying down and not moving on wheels! Mom looked furtively for something to take her mind off her stomach pains. In their suitcase, she found a stuffed bear and the purse Sarah had brought from Lethbridge. When she opened the purse, Sarah saw inside the small gift she had wrapped for Grandma Summers, a gift she would never open.

Sarah began to sob uncontrollably. No tears, just sobs, but at least this new misery had taken her mind off the old one.

Gloria asked Mom where she was going to stay in St. Paul.

"I don't know. We just moved into town."

Without hesitation, Gloria said: "Then you need to come home with us." No questions. No wary glances. It was as if she had been bringing strangers into her home regularly. Just another poor stray.

Both the porter and Gloria had been so kind that neither Mom nor Sarah hesitated to take her up on her offer. Besides, what else could they do?

It was a tiny wood-frame home in the heart of St. Paul's ghetto. As they entered, Sarah couldn't help feeling that she had seen it in a mystery movie. The inside of the house was unbelievably filthy and littered with papers, boxes, and garbage. Some walls had peeling wallpaper or visible cracks in the plaster and others were like a grotesque mosaic of paint patches, torn photos from magazines, and parts of calendars—like a massive collage by Dali or Warhol. Mice were running everywhere, unnoticed by anyone but the new arrivals.

The house had a small porch that appeared so dilapidated that a stiff wind might crumble it. As they entered, the three wanderers walked down a hallway to the kitchen, where Gloria's mother could always be found in her wheelchair, somewhat like a bank guard. To one side was a large bay window, through which she could keep tab on all that was happening out on the street. The hall ended at stairs leading to the bedrooms above. In the parlor were a few pieces of ancient furniture that seemed to be held together only by an invisible force. Against a wall was a dilapidated upright piano whose blanket of dust suggested no one had played it in years. Nevertheless, the parlor was the most used room in the house. The reason Sarah never heard anyone playing the piano was that the television set was on around the clock, day and night, whether anyone was watching or not.

In retrospect, one impression of that house stood out above all others for Sarah. It was eerily dark, mainly because there were very few lights in it and those few were not always turned on at night. Who needed lights when dwellers could be guided by the constant beam cast by the TV set, which droned on and on as if life depended on it? Living in veritable darkness and drawn shades would be a condition Sarah was to experience several years later when her Decade of Horror began in Seattle. But the circumstances would be painfully different.

They would stay at Gloria's house only three weeks, but by the time they departed, it seemed more like a lifetime. Mom and Sarah had never associated with blacks in Canada, and neither one was racially prejudiced. They didn't know what that was. But those three weeks were a supreme test of their tolerance, as was the ghetto itself, Sarah soon learned. For her, one of the problems was Gloria's mother, Mrs. Taylor, an extraordinarily large woman, who had been imprisoned in her wheelchair because she had lost both legs to severe diabetes. Why she took an instant dislike to Sarah, the young girl never discovered, but Mrs. Taylor was kind to little Marian and to Mom. In Marian's case, Sarah remembers being told later that black people are fond of blonde women and have a warm feeling for blonde children. Was it fact or myth? Darkhaired Sarah knew instinctively that it was the latter.

Gloria's mother immediately favored Marian and took her into the kitchen to eat meals with her, while Sarah was clearly told that she was to eat alone in the dining room. That's where she ate all her meals the entire three weeks, while the family, plus blonde Marian, always ate together in the kitchen, sometimes with Mom when she was not out working.

Sarah kept telling herself it was because she was such an ugly child. And she was. Her nose had been broken twice before she was 11, once on a 2-by-4 that she had rammed into nose first when she was 7 and the second time two years later, when she walked into a swinging baseball bat in the neighborhood at Lethbridge. Both injuries healed, but they left her with a prominent nose that haunted her for years and put her on the defensive all of her early life. She also believed her Cyrano-like nose was an important factor in shaping her thoughts, her actions, her fears, and her outlook.

While Mrs. Taylor's doting fondness for Marian was irritating, it did provide an advantage. Because she appointed herself as Marian's sitter, Sarah was relieved of that duty, giving her some time to herself when she returned from school.

The visitors were assigned to an upstairs bedroom. The room had one bed and all three of them slept in it for the three weeks they were there. Besides Gloria's mother, an aunt and a younger sister also lived in the house.

Sarah slept fitfully every night in that house, which made sleeping three in a bed that much more uncomfortable and worrisome. If only she could block out everything else and get some rest. Even bad dreams were preferred to the reality of daily life. Dad was nowhere near the St. Paul ghetto, but Sarah could not banish the fear he had planted in her in Lethbridge. She was a light sleeper, then, by habit and bad memories.

The year was 1966, a turbulent time of race riots in most major American cities, including the Minneapolis-St. Paul area. Mom and her two girls were among the few white families living in the St. Paul ghetto at the time. Because she had to, Mom worked fast. She found a job as a switchboard operator and Sarah was enrolled at the neighborhood school. Sarah and the teacher were the only white persons in the classroom of 32 pupils.

The newcomer from Canada got along well with the boys and most of the girls, but a group of six rebellious girls made life miserable for her, because, they made very clear, she was white and "different." The first week she was at school she was in the girls' toilet one day when the six grabbed a screaming black girl, who was too small to defend herself, and stuffed her into a garbage can. They had pulled her earrings out, and one of them produced a large scissors to cut her hair while the others held her down. It was frightening. Sarah quickly ran out before they could turn on her. But she was marked because she had witnessed their mischief.

One day they approached her and asked if she wanted to play with them. They were smiling, so naïve Sarah took heart and suspected nothing. They took her to the playfield of another elementary school several blocks away. It was a weekend, and no one else was on the school grounds.

As if on cue, they jumped her and "beat the crap out of her," as they themselves described it. They used sticks, rocks, anything they could find, and they kicked her into a faint. Her body was bleeding, but her pride and feelings were hurt much more. Besides, she had once again retreated into her now familiar "other world," her out-of-body existence, so the pain was easier to endure. Only her nose was uninjured. After all, what more could they do to that? Her nose had grown faster than her body. Worst of all, she thought they had beaten her not so much because she was "whitey," but because she was an ugly duckling and had "spied" on their mugging in the girls' toilet.

The punishment would have been even greater in subsequent days had it not been for a tall, black, muscular boy in her class, who seemed always to be smiling.

His name was Stanley, and she would never forget him. For some reason, he took a liking to her and decided he was going to be her bodyguard. Stanley had heard what had happened, and he had no affection for the six girls who had attacked her and who threatened even greater beatings whenever they found her alone. Thanks to him and to school authorities, Sarah was permitted to leave school 15 minutes early and arrive 15 minutes late to avoid the gang of girls or anyone else who fancied making a punching bag of the new white girl.

Stanley was 11, too, and in the same classes as Sarah. He made sure that whenever Sarah had to go to the bathroom, he would escort her to the door, wait till she came out, and escort her back to the classroom or wherever she had to be. At the noon hour, he'd take her to the lunchroom and they would eat lunch together.

He remains one of the wonderful mysteries of her life. She doesn't know why he appointed himself as her guardian and bodyguard. It couldn't have been a physical attraction, because Sarah's unruly hair and overgrown nose were enough to frighten off both males and females. He was polite and softspoken, and he never made any advances nor touched her in any way.

Sarah never saw nor heard anything about him after leaving the ghetto school. She has thought about him often and wished she could say "thank you" to him for coming along at the right time to rescue a frightened little girl. One more thing he did for her: He showed her at just the right time how kind and considerate black people can be, and he solidified a tolerance in her for all minorities that never waivered.

Sarah told Mom about the beating the six girls had given her, and the only advice offered was that Sarah had to be careful and stay away from them. Her message was to "hang on just a bit longer, Sarah Dawn, because brighter days are ahead."

Some consolation that was. Sarah could see immediately that Mom had the same fears she had when she asked her, please, could she get her ears pierced so she could wear earrings.

"Absolutely not! Don't you know that if you wear earrings, someone could come along and rip them off and take some of your ears with them?"

Mom didn't say the gang of girls would do something like that to her, but Sarah knew that's what she was thinking. With the memory of that poor screaming girl in the girls' toilet and the sight of her earrings being forcefully removed, slicing her lobes, Sarah offered no resistance to Mom's warning.

Mom found an apartment for the threesome the fourth week in St. Paul. The only trouble was that it was in the same ghetto area and wouldn't solve Sarah's problem with the Gang of Six. But, thanks to Stanley, the girls stayed away from her in the hallways and in the schoolyard. He never told her why, but Sarah suspected he had read the riot act to those girls and made some suggestions about what might happen to them if they beat her up again.

The new living quarters weren't much of an improvement, but at least the three could keep their two upstairs rooms clean and the way they wanted them. It was a large, old house that had been converted into apartments, and it showed clear signs of terrible workmanship. But at least they were on their own at last. One of the rooms was a small kitchen and the other a bedroom. Once again, all three had to sleep in one bed. Down the hall was a common bathroom that served all second-floor apartment dwellers. Among the tenants on the first floor were a deaf couple with two children and a Basset Hound. They were white and very kind to Sarah. In the months she lived there, she spent a lot of time playing with the children and learning the rudiments of sign language. Although the parents were deaf, the children could speak. They helped teach Sarah what compassion and love in a family could be. What a quaint idea!

Down the hall on the second floor was another boarder, a very attractive, young black woman in her early 20s, who was pleasant and warm the few times Sarah saw her in the hallway or at the bathroom everyone used. In the evenings, the noise from her apartment was excessively loud and constant. She was obviously a party girl, but Sarah never saw who went in or out of her apartment. Not long after the three Summerses moved in, she was found murdered, stabbed to death. Neither the police nor anyone else asked Mom or Sarah any questions nor even their names. It was apparently a case that everyone would just as soon file and forget. That was life in the St. Paul ghetto. The young girl had been heard quarreling with someone with a deep male voice. But no one could identify him. No one saw him. Marian and Sarah had been home the night of the murder, but they saw no one and never left their apartment.

Mom had been out that evening with a friend from Illinois, who had visited her that weekend. When she returned late that night, she nearly panicked:

"How could I have left my children alone in the apartment with a murderer running loose just a few feet away!"

But whenever Sarah asked a question about who committed the murder and why, mum was the word with Mom.

In her family, questions of that kind were met with "We don't talk about such things." In other words, they never talked about important things. They didn't talk about their feelings, their beliefs, their wishes, their hopes, their desires. Sarah soon realized it was the reason that humor, forced or natural, dominated whenever the family was together. Keep 'em laughing and they won't have time for questions about what really matters. Humor was a barricade against the truth and the reality of life. She was sure the reason for the escape to humor was to insulate all of them from the pain that existed in the family over the years.

Mom had to continue leaving the apartment each day for her job at the insurance company's switchboard, but she asked neighbors to watch over the girls. Sarah was practically a prisoner in that apartment, which was equipped with a double door lock.

She pondered her predicament: She had made a transition from daily contact with a Grandmother who loved her and introduced her to the beauty in life to a cruel, ugly environment in which oppressed people made life brutal and dangerous for themselves and everyone else. It was a sad existence for an 11-year-old girl, who had loved to go outdoors and play but who was now trapped on the inside as well as the outside in the world of an urban prison. Had it not been for Stanley, she might not have made it through those nine months in that St. Paul ghetto.

Marian and Sarah existed on a strange diet those days. The three weeks they were at Gloria's house, Sarah consumed nothing but tomato soup and baloney sandwiches day in and day out, and she believed Marian had the same thing, even though she was privileged to eat in the kitchen with Mrs. Taylor. When they moved into their own apartment, Sarah had to fend for Marian and herself as best she could on the frugal means at her disposal. With Mom working full time and being away so much, she would leave Sarah with a few coins each day.

She became a regular customer at the White Castle nearby and could get at least five hamburgers for a quarter—and more when they had special sale days. How she loved those burgers! But she had to admit that after seven or eight months of them as a steady diet, her enthusiasm for the White Castle waned.

Her spirit finally broke the following summer, when she left the grade school and was now ready for a new experience in the junior-high school. In her last week at the grade school, the children were taken on a field trip to visit the junior-high school they were to attend.

At first Sarah was happy to be moving on to a new school, but when she saw it, she decided there was no way she was going to go to that school and stay in the ghetto. The walls of the school, inside and out, were covered with graffiti, foul words, and spray paint of all colors. She tried to walk down the hall of the first floor, but everywhere she went, she was pushed and sneered at. Once more she heard the familiar shouts: "Honky! White bitch! Whitey! Whore!" She couldn't find one white face in the halls or out on the school grounds. And there was no Stanley to protect her this time. Sarah went home terrified. Once again the terrible thought of suicide entered her mind. That night she screamed to her mother:

"I can't do it! I won't do it! I want to leave this place! I will not live here one more day! I'll kill myself if we stay here!"

Mom liked her job at the insurance company and was making strides there. But she was also aware that Sarah was becoming a mental case at school and in the neighborhood. At the same time, the constant turmoil and devastation in the ghetto had its effect on mother and both daughters. The tenement houses had horrible brown yards filled with old, useless cars, damaged bikes and rusted bike parts, and overflowing or toppled garbage cans everywhere. It didn't help Mom's morale when she discovered that the game the girls were sent out to take part in consisted of beating a huge rat to death with a baseball bat. Mom also realized that Marian was now old enough to go to school and would be thrust into the same hell Sarah had been complaining about.

That did it. Mom made a decision on the spot to leave St. Paul and move to Seattle to be with her brother, Sarah's Uncle Roy, who had invited Mom to go there many times. Two days later Mom announced in that same matter-of-fact voice that she had been in touch with her brother and that they should start packing for the move to Seattle. Even the thought of another horrible train ride with motion sickness and three days of throwing up didn't dampen Sarah's delight in knowing that they would be leaving St. Paul.

Tempering Sarah's excitement was a regret that Stanley and the other black children would have to stay behind in the ghetto. That brief period of her life didn't turn her against blacks. Instead it had a reverse effect and created in her a strange sadness and sympathy for them. Like her and her flights from reality through out-of-body experiences to free herself from pain, they must have grown immune to the pain of urban living because they were stranded in ghettos that were not of their own making—de facto prisoners in a country that should be the world's showplace of freedom.

Sarah could relate with them, because she was an underdog, too. Indirectly, those young black children and other minorities she met along the way in her early years showed her the tragedy and pain of prejudice. She wept for them, as she would weep for herself—that is, if only she had the ability to produce tears.

CHAPTER 4

The night before the departure from St. Paul, a mini-tornado ripped through the city. Windows rattled and dogs howled. Flying debris rapped windows and sirens played a steady obbligato to the sound of driving rain and wind. Two trees in front of the Summers' apartment house were ripped from their roots and strewn across the yard, narrowly missing the building.

Sarah was terrified. Was it an omen? Would she ever be able to leave the city that had provided so many distasteful memories? She sobbed all night—so hard that she doesn't remember when the storm finally subsided. The next day they arose and packed the few belongings they had. Whether it was from lack of sleep or the trauma of facing another hurdle in her hectic childhood, Sarah was in a daze and doesn't recall getting aboard the train. It was yet another out-of-body retreat from pain.

She was sure it was her brown pet mouse, Velvet, that brought her back to consciousness. Velvet, successor to Sarah's white mouse, Chi Chi, was the one thing Mom permitted her to take with her on the train. The mouse had been her constant companion, except when she went to school, where pets of any kind were forbidden. The Gang of Six probably would have swiped Velvet from her. If they dared, that is, because Sarah had been told that black people were terrified of mice. Another myth? Of course.

Whenever she went shopping with Mom, she'd take Velvet with her and hide her on the back of her neck so she could cavort in and out of the long hair she wore in those childhood days. Every once in a while, the mouse would dart out of her hair, twitch her nose, and sit up in a begging position on Sarah's shoulder or arm.

She loved the playful mouse, and so did Mom, but when Velvet would pop out from under her long hair at the grocery checkout counter, the clerk invariably would be terrified and summon the manager. Never a dull moment.

Sarah kept Velvet in a shopping bag on the train, and let her out frequently when the porter wasn't around and fed her or played with her. Other passengers seemed to get a kick out of it and smiled indulgently at the antics of both mouse and child. But not so the porter or conductor. They were alarmed when they spotted the mouse, but they didn't know what they could do about it, because their training hadn't covered such situations. They tried to shrug it off, pretending they hadn't seen a thing. Besides, what could they do about it? Sarah had heard the old song, "Throw Mama From the Train a Kiss," but never "Throw Mama From the Train a Mouse."

Mom had arranged to stop over in Havre for three weeks to visit her mother, a visit Sarah didn't look forward to, because that Grandma, Grandma Yoakim, was always crabby and grouchy and clearly showed Sarah she didn't like her. The only thing they had in common was that Grandma despised Sarah's father, too.

Grandma was just as crabby and grouchy as usual throughout the three weeks. That's all Sarah could remember about the uncomfortable visit, although Mom seemed to enjoy herself. In fact, Sarah could recall very little that happened on the trip to Havre, mainly because of her penchant for blocking out unpleasant and threatening episodes in her life.

It was as if Sarah had arrived in another world when the band of three arrived in Seattle, thanks mainly to the glorious green landscape of the Pacific Northwest and the warm greeting of Uncle Roy, who had always been Sarah's favorite relative, despite his love of the bottle. He was her favorite after Grandma Summers, of course. Uncle Roy and his wife drank heavily and often. They were party people—parties every weekend. There it was again, the family hallmark. The curse of alcohol at virtually every turn.

Compared to the ramshackle homes Sarah had lived in back in Lethbridge and St. Paul, Uncle Roy's home was a mansion—a beautiful, huge, family-type house on Seattle's storied Capitol Hill, close by St. Mark's Cathedral. But if it hadn't been for Uncle Roy and his son, Johnny, her month-long stay there would have been another disaster. He and Johnny treated Mom, Marian, and Sarah warmly and were always helpful and considerate. But it was obvious that Aunt Barbara and her three daughters resented their presence as a great intrusion on their lives, which, in fact, it was. They were specially unkind to Sarah. There it was again. Was it her ugly "unprepossessing visage" that haunted her once more?

At any rate, Johnny got along famously with Mrs. Summers, as most people did. He was kind and thought-provoking, even though Sarah felt his liberal ideas were out of line. But, she thought, that would be curbed in time. Unfortunately, he didn't have much time. Johnny died tragically at a very young age, a drowning victim.

His sisters, who were in their subteens or younger, would have nothing to do with Sarah and Marian. The new arrivals had rags and little else, but Aunt Barbara's girls were clothes horses and had everything they wanted, courtesy of an indulgent, arrogant mother. When their parents were away—which was often because both worked during the day—they smoked and drank. Like father and mother, like daughters. Perhaps they weren't aware that they were following family "tradition."

Sarah couldn't understand why Aunt Barbara disliked her so much, even though she attributed all antagonism to her big nose, uneven teeth, and weed-like hair in those days. On one occasion, her aunt scolded her severely for calling her "Aunt" Barbara, which was what Mom told her she should call her. "Aunt" made her feel older than she was, Barbara complained, but Sarah felt the real reason was that she didn't want anyone to know they were related.

The continuing friction undoubtedly had a lot to do with the move by Mom and the two girls a month later to a house owned by Aunt Barbara's mother. It was clear that Sarah's aunt had engineered the move to get the three of them out of her house. However, it was a move that benefited both factions. The house was also in the Capitol Hill District, but far enough removed from Sarah's three cousins, who had treated her as if she were Cinderella—with a protruding nose and no fairy godmother. What a relief!

At last, they were in a comfortable home that suited them well and would give them the fresh start they needed. Sarah knew they were making progress, because she finally had her very own bed and had to share it with no one.

The claustrophobia Sarah had endured in St. Paul was gone at last. Now she could romp in the glorious outdoors whenever she pleased in that gorgeous neighborhood atop one of Seattle's Seven Hills. And, "Saints above us," as Grandma Summers used to say, she could romp, at last, without fear of a beating for a small reason or no reason at all.

Sarah was enrolled at Hamilton Middle School and began to blossom as a student for the first time in her life, because a terrible weight had been lifted from mind and soul. Mom found a job as a phone operator at the University of Washington, and she, too, seemed to breathe easier, smile more, and relax, probably for similar reasons. In no time at all, she brought home a cat given her by one of her friends at work. And why not? Back in Lethbridge, the family had always had cats in the house, sometimes four or five of them. Never dogs.

Sarah couldn't understand why the family never had a dog. At any rate, she was jealous of Mom's cat, which was a Siamese and absolutely precious as a pet. So she had to get her own. By great coincidence, she was playing outside the house one day when she heard a distressed "Meeow" coming from a very tall and very old fir tree. She, too, was a Siamese and all brown. Sarah tried to coax her to come down, but Mom eventually had to call the fire department to help. Doesn't everybody? They put an ad in a Seattle newspaper's lost-and-found columns, and when no one claimed the cat after a couple of weeks, she became Sarah's.

She was named Tiki for no special reason. Sarah chose the name because it just seemed to suit the brown feline—also for no special reason. Do you have to have a reason to name a derelict cat, or any cat, for that matter? Sarah used to play catch with her, and she would amaze the young girl with her ability to hold on to the ball tossed to her. Sarah believed Tiki's previous owner must have been a ballplayer and taught her how to play ball. Or maybe she was a circus cat.

At Hamilton Middle School, Sarah reveled in learning. In St. Paul, she discovered a great difference between the grade schools there and the schools she had known in Canada. What she was given to learn in the sixth grade in St. Paul she had already learned in the second and third grades in Lethbridge. In Canada, she read constantly and couldn't keep her hands off books. Mom said she had a mind like a steel trap. She loved to learn. But when she had entered the oppressive ghetto environment in St. Paul, all ambition to learn vanished and the need for survival was the first and only goal.

At the Seattle school, however, the craving for learning returned, bolstered by teachers like Kent Kammerer, who was the art instructor. He saw that Sarah had talent and a lot of enthusiasm at drawing and took her under his wing.

She would always remember her first achievement, an acrylic plate. With Mr. Kammerer's encouragement, she painted a wetlands scene, complete with cattails, bushes, trees, flowers, and a pond, and he and Sarah ran it through the classroom press, and out came a piece of art! Of course, it was no masterpiece, but it was hers. All hers! They entered it in a competition. It won no prizes, but it traveled in an exhibition from state to state. Imagine that! Only 12, but something she had created was on exhibition in every state in the Union! Who needed a prize?

She was also a good math student but terrible in the language arts. In those two areas, she would never change a bit over the years. It didn't matter then. Sarah was so much in love with school that her morale soared as never before. Mom loved her job at the university and they were getting along like pals again.

Mom also started dating, and the diminished family began living the normal life the three of them had never enjoyed in Lethbridge and St. Paul. Mom's date, a man named Marvin, was divorced and had custody of his two children, and Sarah and Marian grew fond of him and the youngsters, who were younger than they were. But Marvin had one failing: He drank too heavily. He had proposed to Mom, but she turned him down, because she had too vivid a memory of her first marriage and what had turned it sour.

It was during that period that Sarah did something to Mom that she always regretted. Marvin and his children had a pet rat, all white, named Boots, which they left with Sarah on occasion. One night Mom was lying face down on the living-room couch and had dropped off to sleep. She was in her nightgown and robe. Sarah had Boots on her lap and on an impulse she can't explain pulled up Mom's nightgown and robe and let Boots go. When Boots got to her buttocks, Mom awoke with a scream:

"Oh, my God!"

Frightened, Boots urinated all over Mom, then scurried down her legs to the couch and to the floor.

Mom was furious and grounded Sarah for two weeks. But, characteristically, she didn't spank her at a time she certainly deserved it. Perhaps it was because she had learned long ago that beatings solve nothing but create many more problems.

If only Dad had learned that lesson....

Sarah was about 16 when Mom had a call from Dad, who had just discovered she was living in Seattle. He told her he was about to put Sarah's brother, Steve, in a mental institution because of his violent behavior. Mom talked him out of it—perhaps for the first time in her life—and asked him to send Steve to live with her.

In a way, Sarah was happy at the thought of seeing her brother again, even though both Mom and Sarah knew there could be trouble ahead. When they had last seen Steve in Canada, he was a very chubby 10-year-old, who was playful and mischievous but not a problem child. Sarah couldn't believe her eyes when she saw him slither off the bus. Now 15, he was tall and unnaturally thin, with long hair and blackened eyes. And he was visibly angry and bitter. Steve had become a drug and alcohol addict, as the family curse seized yet another victim. And little wonder. Dad had beaten him brutally over the years.

Mom tried hard to steer him into a normal life and to return to school. But it was a hopeless task. In a matter of days, he started skipping school and alienating everyone he met, from teachers to students and others who crossed his path. The drug habit grew worse. Within a few months, Mom had to call police to stop another of his wild, violent streaks, and he was committed to the youth center. Another young victim of child abuse had paid the price—and at only 15 years of age. He was in and out of the center, which was nothing more than a jail for wrongdoers under 18.

Steve eventually became involved with a notorious drug dealer. He had other problems, as well. Almost every day that Sarah returned from school in mid-afternoon, he was in an upstairs bedrom with a girl. The smell of dope was thick and nauseating. When Mom would get home from work, he was still up there, stoned and incoherent.

The few years of relative peace they had enjoyed was now shattered by Steve's continuing troubles. At the same time, Sarah found new obstacles at the high school she was now attending. She could not find acceptance at school because of the way she looked. Her frizzy hair, protruding teeth, and bulging nose seemed to become more prominent as she grew, and both girls and boys at school delighted in taunting her. They laughed uproariously when one of them said she looked like a female Tiny Tim, who was popular at the time. The tag stuck, and she was branded as a Tiny Tim look-alike thereafter.

Sarah searched for ways to turn the tide, to get fellow students at least to let her join their inner circle, but nothing worked. In fact, the harder she tried, the nastier the insults and derisive laughter became. It seemed that most of the students were into drugs heavily, so Sarah thought she should try them to be accepted. Her first experience was with speed, but she hated it. Then she tried acid and thought she was rapidly losing her mind. Next she "went with the crowd" and tried beer, then wine—lots of it. And she got so sick she thought she'd never recover.

All were easy to obtain, whether it was speed, acid, alcohol, or some of the things Sarah never tried, like crack or heroin. One more thing she didn't try at the time was sex, even though most of the other students were doing so, and often.

In the midst of her new dilemma, she thought once again of committing suicide. Trying to be "in" hadn't won her any friends, and her refusal to have sex turned the boys against her. It wasn't hard for her to discontinue toying with drugs and alcohol, mainly because they made her so ill she couldn't take them any more. But it was hard for her to hide the face nobody could love. In her desperation, the idea of ending her life kept coming back as an alternative.

Sarah was walking by a small shop near the school grounds one day and saw her reflection in a mirror inside the window. As she peered into the glass to examine herself, she could hear her inner voice saying:

"Who would ever love me? Why would I ever be worthy of someone's love?"

The real question was one she didn't think of at the time: "Why hadn't I learned to love myself—love myself for what I was?"

Sarah would have to go through hell on earth a bit later in her life before she realized that she had to discover and respect herself before she could expect others to love her and care about her.

She would discover that it was difficult to say you love yourself when you don't grow up in an environment in which people teach you and show you how to appreciate yourself for who you are. Instead, you keep looking outside yourself for a personna you think others will like and even love. It just doesn't work. Sarah would learn that that was the reason so many women were in the desperate positions they created for themselves. They are so busy being someone else that they forget to be themselves and accept it.

The returning thought of suicide swept Sarah once again into that now familiar out-of-body feeling, and she was saved—from herself. But this time the suicidal impulse prompted her to want to do something about her facial appearance. A switchboard friend of Mom's had a daughter who had just had plastic surgery to reduce the size of her nose, and the friend recommended that Sarah see the doctor. He was Dr. Walter Scott Brown, a black surgeon, who had become notorious not only for reshaping noses but for giving chorus girls and burlesque dancers larger busts. At the time Sarah visited him, Dr. Brown was quite old and getting around on crutches.

"OK, Darlin'," he said cheerily, "what kind of nose do you want? You can have a Roman nose, a ski-jump nose, or a fat nose."

Sarah thought she had died and gone to heaven!

"I want a ski-jump nose, please."

"Well," he said, stroking his chin, "that will be a little harder, because you have somewhat of a long nose. But we'll see what we can do."

Mom quickly made the arrangements. They decided to do it at the Christmas break, because school would be out and Sarah knew she'd have black-and-blue marks for a while. The surgery was performed on December 22, and it was very, very painful. It didn't matter how much he numbed Sarah, she couldn't get numb. Where was her out-of-body escape when she needed it most?

Pain or no, Dr. Brown went ahead with the surgery anyway, and she certainly felt it when he did it.

"Now this is going to sound worse than it hurts," he said as he picked up a small chisel, inserted it into her nose, then struck it with a hammer.

Her entire nose seemed to have shattered, and she thought she was about to die. She could feel it and she could see it. Too late for an out-of-body retreat. A rather husky nurse held her down, and Sarah understood why he had hired a muscular assistant.

"Let's go for it!" he said, as he reset Sarah's nose, then packed it. It took a relatively short time, but the packing hurt so much she had to stay in the hospital overnight. On Christmas Day, Dr. Brown removed the packing and she heaved a gigantic sigh of relief. He was kind, patient, and always trying to make her smile. And what an incredible Christmas gift he had given her.

She couldn't praise him enough. He had given her back her hope and her life. But for the time being, Sarah looked hideous, and that's the way she would be for several months afterward. When she returned to school after Christmas vacation, other students—the males particularly—taunted her: "Hey, Summers, did you get a nose job or something over the Christmas break?" It was always followed by a loud laugh.

It took a year for her nose and face to look normal. In that time, she changed her hair style drastically to suit the new profile. The nose Dr. Brown gave her was a Roman nose, not the ski-jump variety she had asked for, but she understood that he had no choice.

Needless to say, the boys eventually paid more attention to her after she said farewell to Tiny Tim.

She thanked God that she didn't have to adopt the repulsive drug-and-alcohol routine to be noticed any more. One boy in particular, Don Brady, caught her attention. He was handsome and had big blue eyes and blond curly hair. A dreamboat, the girls would say. Sarah lost her head over him, but it didn't last. It was Don who provided her with her first sexual experience, and the fact that it didn't go very well accounted for their decision to break up the budding romance.

Sarah had thought her first experience would be a beautiful, heavenly event. But nothing happened. He tried hard and may have enjoyed it, but she felt no pleasure, no ecstasy, no passion. What was wrong with her? She had not had an orgasm, nor did she come close to having one. Lord, how she wanted so much to swoon with rapture and explode in sexual pleasure, but she lay there waiting, waiting, waiting. Was that all there was to love and sex? At first, she thought it was Don who might have been responsible for not arousing her in the slightest. But that seemed unlikely. He had been patient and loving. Now she had a new worry. Was her out-of-body protection against pain also a barrier against pleasure? What was wrong with her mind and body?

Somehow she got through high school and received a diploma. But she had approached graduation without excitement or even interest. The reason was she had no idea where her life would take her, because she had no incentives.

Sarah had shown considerable talent in art at school and wanted to make it her life's work, possibly as a commercial artist. Besides, Mom had told her often that she admired her art work.

But when she told Mom she wanted to enroll in a private art school for career training, Mom said: "If you want to go to art school, you'll have to do it on your own. I want you to know there's no way in the world that I am going to pay for that."

Then, uncharacteristically, Mom launched into a barrage about how she had given up her life for Sarah and she wasn't about to do it any longer—and it was time Sarah took care of herself and got a job, instead of thinking about more schooling.... It went on and on. Mom had been holding all those complaints in for so long that her anger grew and grew as she talked.

This wasn't Mom. It couldn't be. But when she finally let it all out, she triggered Sarah's long-guarded feelings, too.

"Please remember that I had no childlhood and no teen-age years, because I always had to be a substitute mother, first to all three kids and then to Marian, while you were out working most of the day and part of the night all those years."

It was the first serious clash they had had, and it left both of them exhausted and full of anger, anger that had been muzzled for years. It was the cause of a break between them that lasted a long time—too long. Both knew they were wrong, but the heat of the moment permitted no apologies.

That disagreement was partly responsible for what happened next. After graduation, David, a very handsome boy Sarah had met at school but who had shown little interest in her before the nose surgery, called and asked for a date. She had had her eye on him for two years at school, but he was much more interested in other girls, preferably easy dates with large breasts. Sarah had dated Don with the hope that it would make David jealous, but it didn't work.

In the process, she had also lost her virginity, although she was so cold to the love-making that she didn't consider it much of a loss, if any at all. She and David hit it off well and in no time they decided to live together. In fact, they lived together on and off for about five years before deciding to get married. She wasn't ready for housekeeping and domestic life with a man, but she didn't want to go back to her previous life either.

Almost from the beginning, her relationship with David was doomed. He, too, was a product of a broken family. Worse yet in his case, his mother was mentally ill and had to be confined to an institution, leaving him to be the caretaker of a younger brother. He and Sarah had too much in common. David hadn't been beaten severely as a boy, but he certainly had been abused emotionally and showed it.

Sarah had a variety of jobs in those years, including secretarial work, part-time receptionist, sales clerk, cleaning homes, and cutting hair, all of them for short periods of time. David was a barber and had a shop in a well-to-do section of Seattle.

When she told David she was going into training at a beauty school and would be gone from the house most days and nights, he shrugged his shoulders in disgust and suggested she plan on leaving. What was she to do?

When, after a few months, the training led to a job in a beauty salon and, finally, a few bucks in her purse, David suggested they get together again. This time they decided to get married.

It was a terrible mistake, but they went through with it anyway. She liked him, but she knew she didn't love him. With him, as with Don, sex was a chore for Sarah, something she had to do because he expected it of her. She was not fulfilled in the sex act at any time with David, and she did not understand why.

Their problems in marriage surfaced quickly. David became hooked on cocaine and alcohol, which soaked up all of his income and much of hers, as well. He had always been a womanizer, but now he began flaunting it, perhaps because he found no gratification with Sarah in the bedroom.

She eventually found out that he had slept with virtually all the feminine friends they had. Their lives together became living hell. His abuse mounted when he was in his cups or on a high. He also began to demand money she didn't have.

That did it. Once more she stared deeply into the tell-tale mirror and said to herself: "I've had it. I need to find a job that will bring in a lot more money. I also don't need this marriage."

Mirrors played an important role in her life because they forced her to look at herself in a way she couldn't accomplish with introspection.

She told David she wanted a separation and a divorce. He offered no resistance. She was 24 at the time. It wasn't necessary yet to leave the house, but that obviously was in the cards in due time. Besides, he spent little time with her and in the house, so a separation of sorts was already in effect.

The worst, by far, was just ahead. If only she had known....

Chapter 5

For most humans, spring promises fresh, new life. But that spring was anything but promising for Sarah. Her brief, passionless marriage was unraveling. She and her mother were not speaking. Her family had crashed on the rocks of alcohol, drugs, and violence. And her ill-advised marriage had depleted what little she had tried to put away in the bank. She had to face the fact that she was broke and had to do something about it pronto. For the first time in her life, she felt alone, desperately and miserably.

All she had left was the notion that she would not starve, because she had learned to cut and shape hair, which she could do at home, and, in a pinch, she knew she could make enough to live on by cleaning homes for the well-to-do, if she had to. But her conscience told her she had to do better than that. What she needed was a steady, well-paying job and some stability. She had to make another stab at those goals before total depression and the suicidal impulse returned.

In addition, Mom had given her an ultimatum after she graduated from high school. She could live at home for a minimum of one year, but after that, she had to move out. Among the many odd jobs she tried in that furtive year were positions at a downtown department store, including waitressing at the sandwich shop, selling in the lingerie section, and clerking in the office. None of the jobs offered her any stability or a future, but fortunately one of the jobs brought her into contact with the owner of the city's largest hair-styling emporium, which had several branches, one of them in the department store. When he learned she had some experience in hairstyling, he asked for Sarah's phone number and told her he would be calling her soon.

The salon mogul kept his promise. He called Sarah a few weeks later and offered her a job as a receptionist at one of his branch salons. Fortune seemed to be smiling down at her at last, and she said to herself that maybe, just maybe, this job might be the turning point in her life. It wasn't. At first, she didn't mind the salon-keeper's brusque, bossy behavior, believing it was all part of the breaking-in routine, like the first year at West Point or Annapolis. But his dictatorial attitude got worse, not better, and she told him one day that she didn't like being ordered around like a servant.

He told her he wanted her to report to an associate, who handled all his personnel affairs at another branch salon. The associate wasted no time:

"The boss thinks you're too big for your britches. I'm afraid I have to fire you."

Sarah admitted she had, in fact, been "too big for her britches" and accepted her medicine as if all the fault had been hers. It was then back to the department store for a job selling panties and bras, hardly the stimulating career she had sought. The only solace she had was to tell herself that the arrogant salon owner was a pain in the rear anyway and he liked to flaunt his association with VIPs in town, from football coaches to industrial tycoons, most of whose wives patronized his swank salon. He basked in the limelight supplied by the wealthy socialites and businesswomen who fawned over him and made his salon their second home.

Fate and coincidence then took a hand for Sarah at a time her morale was at its lowest. At the lingerie counter, she saw a young woman she had known briefly at the salon. Penny Watson was a successful hairstylist who worked for the salon boss, and Sarah soon discovered she was one of the most personable and considerate people she had met. Their friendship blossomed quickly and they began trading personal secrets. Sarah soon learned that she, too, had been the victim of a terribly abusive family. They spoke the same language.

One night they were having a cocktail before dinner at a downtown hotel when in walked Mr. Salon King himself. Recognizing them quickly, he suggested they go up to his apartment for more conversation and a drink or two. It was a legitimate pitch for conversation, not hanky-panky, because his wife was in town. Sarah was surprised at his pleasant behavior. He seemed to have forgotten that he had fired her only a couple weeks earlier.

He lost no time. "I always liked you, Sarah, because you have spunk. Besides you weren't in the right job before. If I put you through beauty school, would you come back to work for me?"

To Sarah, it was like a gentleman's confession and honest apology. She accepted. Besides she knew how well off Penny was financially, and the prospect of duplicating her success made her almost giddy. It was as if someone had finally handed her a Hollywood contract.

Sarah quit her department store job and began her training at the beauty school, which, unfortunately, was miles away from home—and she was without a car and couldn't afford to buy one. But she was determined not to blow the new opportunity, because she felt it might be her last chance at a good salary and a decent job. She rose every morning at 5, took a bus to town and transferred to another one crossing the lake to the beauty school in Bellevue. It was at that time that David had blown his stack and told her to pack up and leave.

After her first trimester at the beauty school, she began working nights under the tutelage of the salon chief himself, who insisted on training all of his stylists in his own procedures. It was one of the secrets of his enormous success.

For Sarah, it was one of the most rigorous schedules she'd ever undertaken, but she gritted her teeth and pressed forward. It was rise at 5, spend nearly two hours on busses, a full day in classes at the beauty school, then an hour back to town, and the night shift cutting hair as a novice.

She learned a great deal. The improvement in her technique was so quick and so great that the salon would charge her out to customers at an increasingly higher rate, mainly because she was being trained in the Vidal Sassoon style.

Sarah could cut the geometric cuts and all the rest. However, on graduating from beauty school, she flunked the first board test. It happened because she took a chance and guessed wrong. She thought she would most certainly be tested for procedure on a scissors cut, rather than a razor cut, so she concentrated in her studies and practice on a scissors cut. Nobody, she said to herself, cut hair with razors any more. With her usual luck, she drew the test on the razor cut and flunked.

She had to redo the board tests again a short time later, and this time she passed easily. The entire schooling, testing, and licensing process had taken her nearly two and a half years, but she went to work for the hairdressing baron full time at his show-case salon in downtown Seattle. She worked directly under him and learned to know him well. In her sensitive position, Sarah also learned the latest gossip about the town's leading lights. What a column she could have written for a newspaper! Some of the gossip concerned the boss himself, who had become quite a playboy. It could have been expected for a man who catered to hundreds of the city's wealthiest women.

Then, one day the inevitable happened to Sarah. The girl at the reception desk called back and asked Sarah if she would please go up front to handle "a situation" that had arisen. Becky Stroheim, the wife of one of the city's most influential industrial giants, was throwing her weight around, as usual, and making an embarrassing scene.

"What can I do for you, Mrs. Stroheim?" Sarah asked.

"Who are you?"

"I'm his assistant. Is there anything I can do for you?"

"I want him to blow-dry my hair."

"But he already has two clients waiting and is still working on another. May I do it for you? I frequently work with him, and I'd be glad to blow-dry your hair right away."

Mrs. Stroheim stamped her feet, raised her voice to a shout, and tossed off a few choice four-letter words. It was a first-class tantrum by an unclassy dame. With a few choice descriptions for Sarah, she stalked off toward the salon director's private room and proceeded to berate him with expletives that would have done a longshoreman proud.

"Your bimbo here told me you can't do my hair. I won't have anybody else touch me. You've always taken me on right away. What the hell is going on?"

He shot a glance at Sarah that was like a shaft of acid.

It was a glance that chiseled itself in her memory. If looks could kill, she would have been a corpse right there at the classiest salon in town.

To Mrs. Stroheim, he said in the voice of an obsequious slave: "You know, Becky, I can handle you right away." He grabbed Sarah's arm and pulled her before Mrs. Stroheim and himself, saying in a boiling voice: "Sarah, don't you ever do that again!"

Sarah was boiling, too, but she managed to hide her embarrassment, at least for the moment. He gulped as he asked her to shampoo

Mrs. Stroheim and prepare her for the rest. A few moments later, on a cue from him, Sarah said:

"He's tied up right now with Jane Simpson, the TV anchor woman, and he asked me to do this for you."

Mount Vesuvius erupted a second time.

"I will not have an assistant drying my hair, dammit!"

Something snapped in Sarah's mind. She didn't have to take this crap from anyone, least of all a spoiled bitch who flaunted her wealth and social position. Laying aside the dryer and brush, she managed to say, "Excuse me a moment. I must see Monsieur le Directeur." Sarah marched into his room.

"Sorry, but I must speak with you a moment. Right now!" They walked into his private office.

"Thanks very much for everything, but I will not work under these conditions and take this kind of abuse from Mrs. Rich-Bitch and all the others like her. I'm leaving. Goodbye!"

It was his turn to pop off, but he didn't get much said, because Sarah had already walked out. So much for the "dream job."

Sarah spent another sleepless night, asking herself if she had done the right thing. Her conscience said, "You've blown it again, Sarah. Why can't you hold your tongue and do what you're told?" But her mind said, "Good for you, Sarah. You don't have to swallow that crap from anybody." When was she going to draw some respect and consideration from decent human beings? She wondered if her life of perpetual abuse would ever come to an end.

Bleary-eyed, exhausted, and demoralized, Sarah got out of bed slowly the next morning, wondering why she shouldn't just stay there and await her last breath. Even the warm shower didn't feel good this miserable day. She knew she could work in one of the small beauty shops, because she had several friends there. And that was what she did for a few months, but there was no satisfaction in it any more.

Like it or not, it was back to the newspaper help-wanted ads. One morning she spotted an ad calling for a part-time secretary in a financial-planning firm. Hmmm. Why not? With a part-time job like that, she could continue cutting hair in the evenings or on weekends to replenish her bank book. Besides she no longer had to support David and his drug-and-alcohol habit, so she could be free again.

When she answered the ad, she was interviewed by the owner of the planning firm, Lane Turnbull, a muscular, heavy-set man, who appeared to be in his early 40s. His office was in a onetime hillside home that was spacious and on three levels. There were no lights on in the office, and she noticed that Mr. Turnbull had cracked the blinds just enough for a little bit of light to come through. It was a beautiful spring day and he wore sunglasses, even though he had his back to the window. Strange, but she brushed it all aside, because he was polite and seemed anxious to make her comfortable.

From the very beginning, he insisted that she call him Lane, not Mr. Turnbull. She was disarmed by his pleasant voice and his apparent interest in her job record, her training, and her aspirations, even though the job was part-time and would require her presence from 10 in the morning to 2 Tuesdays through Fridays. The starting pay was only $5 an hour, but it was more than she had been making in the days before the salon experience. Sarah had to spike her dream of instant wealth. Nevertheless, the part-time aspect and the job he outlined were inviting. Besides, what else could she do?

Lane said he was pleased with her credentials, experience, and ability, but before he could offer her the job, he said she had to be interviewed by his wife, Darlene. Sarah went to see her at her specialty store, which was only a few blocks away, and she asked her many questions about her past, her skills, and her ideas on how to improve the office procedure. She did it all without a smile and in matter-of-fact fashion, but she told Sarah she could have the job if Lane approved.

She started the very next day. The first chore Lane assigned her was to organize all his files, which were in shambles, and bring some order to the office, which had obviously been left in great disarray. She didn't discover till much later that the reason for the chaos was twofold: The previous secretary, with whom he had been sleeping regularly the previous five years, had quit in disgust, and Lane himself had been gambling heavily and losing and was in treatment with a therapist, apparently because he had fallen in love with his secretary and she had demanded that he leave his wife.

Darlene either ignored or pretended to know nothing about his paramour, his gambling, or his need for therapy. Or did she? How could she have been kept ignorant of his five-year fling, his quick trips to Reno to play at the tables, and his therapy sessions? Theirs was clearly a marriage of convenience, but Sarah never discovered for sure what it was that kept them together. Her best guess was that Darlene controlled the purse strings in the marriage, because she would some day inherit quite a bit of money. And he didn't want to lose his meal ticket.

At any rate, Sarah was oblivious to all that in the beginning and enjoyed the responsibility of reorganizing the office. It was quite a challenge, and she reveled in it. Besides, Lane was gone most of the time, and his wife was not permitted to interfere in his business. The specialty store she ran occupied most of her time, and she seemed to be disinterested in his work anyway.

At last, Sarah thought, she had found a job with a lot of promise for advancement and the expectancy of good pay. Besides, she could make additional spending money at night as a hairdresser. And she no longer had to worry about wealthy, spoiled dowagers and pushy women. The glamour of working in a plush planning office and running it the way she wished seemed too good to be true. The poor image she had created for herself was beginning to undergo a transformation. Reared in poverty, abuse, and family dysfunction, she would finally have a chance to work and live like a decent human being!

The reverie continued for about two months, and the part-time job soon became a full-time position, which was just fine with Sarah. Her reorganization of the office and many other changes and innovations she brought to office procedure met with instant approval from Lane. He asked her to begin sitting in on presentations made to couples who had come in for financial advice. She was intrigued by the importance of the work and the great impact the consultations seemed to have on their lives.

It was about that time, a few months after taking the job, that Sarah moved out of the house and told David she wanted her freedom. When she informed Lane that she was in the process of splitting with her husband and that she needed to find a new place to live, he said that could be fixed in no time. He found her an apartment just across the street from the office, making it very convenient and inexpensive for her to work there. And, she didn't realize at the time, immensely convenient for him, as well. In her naivete, she was grateful and euphoric. How lucky could she get?

At the time, she was so impressed with Lane's apparent grasp of financial issues, tax laws, and his own theory of managing funds that she had no suspicion that something was awry. Or soon would be.

She made the fatal mistake of telling Lane the details of her life with David, his serious drug and alcohol problems, and her own financial problems. Sarah was broke and needed the job very much.

When Lane said he wanted her to look her best on the job and that she should go out and buy herself a wardrobe worthy of the new job, she told him she couldn't afford it just yet. He immediately took out his checkbook.

"Oh, of course you can't afford it. But here's a check for a thousand dollars, payment in advance. Please take it and go out and buy whatever you need. Get your hair done, too. And if that's not enough, just let me know."

Sarah didn't suspect a thing. She was overwhelmed by his kindness and vowed she would do a super job of running his office.

An incident that should have sounded an alarm in her mind occurred a short time before she left David for good. The basement floor of the planning office had an apartment with bedroom and bath for occasional use by Lane's clients and friends. He asked if she and David wanted to earn a little extra money by painting the entire apartment. They were hard-pressed for money, so they agreed to accept his offer, even though their home life was anything but tranquil at the time.

They started the job on a Sunday afternoon. Sarah remembered it well because of what happened. Lane and Darlene had a young son, Marshall, and he had come along with his mother for some family matter Sarah knew nothing about. However, in the course of their conversation, Lane and Darlene raised their voices in an argument, and Lane suddenly ended the spat by slapping her face so hard she nearly fell. Sarah was more surprised than she was, so she had to surmise it had happened before. Darlene departed in a huff, her son behind her.

That evening, David snarled and said he was surprised that Sarah would want to work for any man who would strike his wife or any woman that way. But Sarah was still in a daze over getting a job with a planning firm that seemed to be so successful and she blurted out:

"I'll bet she deserved it!"

Sarah failed to heed the warning of the slapping incident. A week later, Lane returned from one of his trips and called her into his office.

"What a rotten job of painting! Did you two ever paint a room before? You ought to give me back my money."

Was he kidding? Was this his way of avoiding having to say thanks for a large favor? Sarah wasn't sure, because she knew she and David had done a first-rate job of painting the apartment. Lane didn't press it at the time, but she would soon discover that the incident was not forgotten.

Several weeks earlier, Lane had asked her if she'd like to have a cocktail now and then. Since she and David had been imbibing rather heavily at the time, mainly as an excuse to avoid talking to each other, Sarah said, "Yes. My favorite drink is a Brave Bull, which is tequila and kahlua on the rocks." When she asked why he had brought it up, he said, simply, "Oh, I just wanted to know," and walked away. That's all there was to it.

On a Friday afternoon a short time later, he asked her if she would like to stay and have a friendly drink before winding up the week in the office.

"I have your favorite, tequila and kahlua. Let's drink a toast to another successful week at the office."

He was smiling and friendly. They had a drink, then a second one. He was a perfect gentleman for the hour or so. Not until much later did she learn that he pretended to be drinking but in fact was faking it with a pop drink or an empty glass.

The Friday cocktail hour became a regular feature each week for the next month or two. Then the shoe fell. After a second drink one afternoon, Lane's demeanor changed abruptly.

"I haven't forgotten that lousy painting job you and your husband did, you know. You should give me back the 200 bucks I paid you. And while I'm at it, do you remember the thousand I gave you to buy clothes? I think we need to make an arrangement for you to pay me back."

Sarah was stunned. She didn't have $200 to pay him back. And a thousand was out of the question, since David had drained the last of their resources to keep himself in crack and alcohol.

"Can't you take it out of my future pay?"

"I can't wait that long. I'll tell you what my payment arrangement will be with you. You're going to have sex with me."

For the longest moment, she couldn't say a word. A chill darted through her body. If she defied him, she would undoubtedly be giving up the best job she had held in some time—one that could get her out of her constant predicament of poverty.

All she could think of to say was, "Well, that's not acceptable to me. I'm still married, you know, and I don't want to have that kind of relationship with you."

He wasn't smiling any more. "It doesn't matter. I've got enough information about you now that tells me I can do anything with you that I want. You're married to a guy who sleeps with every broad he can find. He's a cocaine addict and a drunkard, and who is going to believe that you aren't, too?"

She knew she was in a vulnerable position. Her marriage was on the rocks, and Lane knew that. He also knew she had to scramble for every penny she made to survive. And he knew her family had written her off and wouldn't go to her rescue. Lane the Schemer made it his business to know everything about his future victims.

Her head was whirling from the two drinks she had had, drinks he had made doubly strong. And all that time, he was pretending to drink from a bottle of vodka and actually pouring himself 7-Up. Machiavelli could have learned from him.

No longer was there a trace of a smile on his face. He stared at her and said firmly: "You have a financial obligation to me, and this is the way you're going to compensate me. And if you tell anybody about it, I'll make sure that you're the one that looks bad and that it will be reflected permanently in your resume. So, you just think about what you're going to do. I'll set it up and let you know when the payments will start."

It was like a prison sentence. But she was tongue-tied and couldn't protest. He didn't waste any time making the "arrangement." Early the next week, he told her he had clients coming in that weekend and wanted her to work Saturday. He would tell Darlene he had to work late that night and would not be home, and he said Sarah could tell David anything she damn wished—as if that mattered at the time.

In a daze, Sarah went to the office that Saturday to help in the interviews with the clients. When they left, Lane ordered her downstairs, despite her protests.

"Now get undressed!" he ordered like a Prussian colonel.

When Sarah said once more, "I don't want to do this," he replied:

"Either you undress yourself or I'll undress you myself. Make up your mind."

He struck her in the face with the back of his hand.

Good Lord he was strong! She had no choice. What would he do to her if she refused? She felt herself leaving her body, as had happened so many times before with her father before a beating. He was forcing her legs apart and shuffled his heavy body atop hers. It was horrible, even though she had no detailed recollection of what happened from then on. Each time she tried pushing him away, he would deliver a hand to her head. His hands were powerful. Even though she didn't remember the penetration, she screamed with pain. His sex organ was enormous, while hers was unusually small—so small that she had always been afraid she might never be able to bear a child.

She didn't know how long that first encounter lasted, because she had turned the pain off from the start. When he was finished, he got up abruptly, slapped her on the butt, and said nonchalantly, as if nothing unusual had happened:

"OK, take these sheets home with you and wash them. You can return them Monday and make the bed."

Sarah didn't know what he was talking about until she looked down and saw that the sheets were drenched with blood—her blood. He had been so violent that he had torn her up.

If she had been a virgin, she thought, she might have bled to death. She had been raped but couldn't tell anybody about it. Carting a bundle of bedsheets, she got into her car and drove for more than two hours. She can't remember where she went that night, but the tank, which she had filled in the morning, was close to empty when she finally arrived home at 3 in the morning.

The next day, panic-stricken, she called Mom, apologized for not having talked to her for so long, and told her she was about to divorce David. What she really wanted to tell her was that she had just been raped by her employer and needed advice on what to do, but she couldn't get the words out. Instead of receiving sympathy and the advice she so desperately needed, her mother, who had recently remarried, said sternly:

"If you divorce David, you'll also be divorcing your family."

Stunned again, twice in one weekend. Sarah had no one she could turn to—not her mother, husband, sister, brother, father, nor even a close friend. Once again the specter of suicide entered her mind.

If it had happened 20 years later, she would have known what to do and where to go for help. But sexual harassment of women in those days was still a phrase without legal muscle, without public acknowledgment and the political power of American women. At that time, even the term, "comparable worth," was brand new in the legislative halls of the nation and, most certainly, in Congress. The tailhook affair, which struck so strong a blow for the cause of harassed and battered women, was still two decades down the road. In the 1960s, she was trapped by her own afflictions of poverty, loneliness, and even stupidity—a fly in a spider's web.

In her bewilderment, Sarah brushed aside the idea of going to a doctor to check the bleeding. What could he do? He was no cop. Besides, she felt so ashamed for getting herself into the predicament that she didn't want anybody to know how far she had fallen and how little self-esteem she had.

She was painfully naïve. Of course, she had heard and read about rape and violence to women, but, naturally, that could never happen to her, because she never went near dangerous territory. Oh, yeah…!

Like a zombie, Sarah went to work the next week, hoping she would not have to face him. She had washed the sheets, out of fear more than anything else, and had returned them to the bed in the downstairs apartment. Her mind was busy plotting how she would get out of this dilemma and still keep her job. She was jarred from her trance by his cheery voice:

"Well, now, how's my girl? I see you've done what I asked you to do and that everything is in order. Good girl."

Lord! A compliment from the devil himself when she was dying inside. He was smiling as if nothing had happened. How could this rapist pretend to be so cheerful?

She doesn't know why she said what she did: "Yeah, thanks for everything. You cut me to ribbons, dammit. The least you could have done was wear a condom."

"Don't have to, Sweetie. I had a vasectomy several years ago. I'm off the hook, and so are you."

If a gun had been handy, she'd have committed murder at that moment. Vasectomy? How dare he! This monster was a menace to all women and didn't deserve to go on breathing.

Chapter 6

If Sarah had any doubts about Lane's intention to pursue his evil course, they were soon dispelled. After her brutal initiation in his bedroom, his attitude toward her changed drastically. No longer was there a pretense of a smile or a kind word. The gentle, considerate treatment she had received from him the first few months on the job disappeared.

It had all been a sham, a come-on for what only he knew was ahead. Now she was treated like a slave, subject to whatever whims possessed him; she also became his resident punching bag. The demands for sex now came frequently, as often as two or three times a week. And all she could do was retreat more deeply into the shell of her out-of-body existence to ward off the pain.

He began grabbing her by the neck and slapping her whenever she displeased him or didn't perform in the office or in the bedroom to his liking. At first they were light slaps, but in time they became vicious—hard cracks across the face and chin that sent her reeling. They were frequently accompanied by disdainful words:

"You stupid whore! You're the most incompetent fucking bitch I've ever met in my life! You don't do anything right. I'm sick and tired of your fuckups. What are you going to do about it? Tell me. What are you going to do about it?"

At first, she said nothing. But that only infuriated him more, and he'd grab her by the neck or arm and squeeze hard to get a reaction. Later, she tried to placate him by lying, saying she had screwed up and that she was sorry and that it wouldn't happen again. It worked for a while, but in time nothing could ward off his abuse.

Sometimes he would threaten her with more than his fists. He had a large gun collection in the office and would frequently take one of the weapons out and aim it at an object somewhere in the room. He would turn slowly, point a gun directly at her head, and say:

"One of these days, I'm..." He never finished the sentence, but there was no mistaking his threat.

When he was specially angry with her, he would grab her by the throat with both hands, lift her body, and slam her up against the wall, then slowly relax his grip. She never knew which episode would be her last.

Early one morning, Lane walked into the office and said:

"Come on. Get your duds on. We're going out to see Mort. I'm going to teach you how to shoot a gun."

She had no interest in firing a gun or anything else, but he would accept no excuse. He took several pieces out of his gun cabinet and ushered her out of the office to his car.

Mort had visited Lane in the office on several occasions, but she had never had a conversation with him and knew very little about him. He was a gun salesman and always brought a large case full of weapons into the office, because Lane was a good customer.

They drove more than an hour north of Seattle to a winding dirt road that led to an open field. There they met Mort. He looked just as Sarah had remembered him on his visits to the office. Even to his clothes. He wore the same trench coat, dark pants, dark turtle-neck sweater, and dark shoes. His short, dirty, sandy-blond hair was almost a buzz cut. Lean and tall in contrast to the stocky Lane, he had pocked skin and his eyes were greenish-gray. She never felt comfortable in his presence and wished she were some place else when he trained those penetrating eyes on her. He didn't wear a hat, but he frequently wore sunglasses that appeared to be part of his face—as if he were linked to Lane in some kind of underground brotherhood. His speech was short and clipped. He never said more than he had to. When he took off his sunglasses indoors, his eyes penetrated her like a hot sword.

"Whenever I think of him, I'm reminded of walking death, as if he had no soul. He seemed to be a Darth Vader living on earth."

Mort had set up some bottles, cans, and other makeshift targets about 400 or 500 feet from where the three of them stood in the field. That day they were firing .38s, 357s, and 44 Magnums. Lane insisted on showing her how to shoot. He said it would be good for her to learn and to carry her own weapon in case she had to defend herself. Sarah couldn't understand why he made the suggestion. Wouldn't she then be a danger to him….?

With Lane standing behind her, she tried all three weapons he had brought, and she was surprised at how well she did. She was no sharpshooter, but she hit the target frequently. Each time she shot, Lane would brace himself against her to help absorb the recoil. When she had gone through a few rounds, he picked up the weapons himself. She was not surprised to see what a good shot he was.

Then it was Mort's turn. Sarah and Lane had had many misses, but not Mort. He was a fantastic marksman. No matter what the distance of the target, he never missed a single one, and her recollection is that he fired off at least three or four dozen rounds. When he finally put down the weapons, Lane gave Sarah a look that sent shivers down her spine. He saw that she was clearly impressed with Mort's shooting.

They said goodbye to Mort and drove off to return to the city. Before they had gone 100 yards back down the dirt road, Lane said to her, coldly and without looking at her:

"I want you to remember what you saw today. Do you know what Mort does for a living?"

"I know he sells guns, but I had no idea he was such a great shot."

Lane paused a moment, then said, still not looking at her: "He's an assassin. He gets paid to kill people. If you ever tell anybody about our relationship, Mort will take care of you."

Sarah swallowed hard and pretended she hadn't heard. "Pardon me?"

"You heard exactly what I said."

A minute went by as she froze in her seat, terrified. Then, as if he had said nothing important, Lane smiled that phony smile of his and asked, as if nothing unusual had happened:

"Are you hungry for lunch? Shall we get something to eat?"

As if her life had not already dealt her more than her share of foul blows, now she had to worry about an assassin's bullet if she didn't do her master's bidding. Sarah was trapped as never before. Even the thought of going to the police vanished from her mind. It could cost her her life. First she had been blackmailed for $1,200, and now she had to live each day in mortal fear, because there was a hit man out there waiting for orders....

Lane took over her life. Why didn't she escape and run off to a different environment and maybe even another city far away from Seattle?

It was that same old fear of losing the first important job she'd ever had—and now, in addition to that, she feared being tracked down and murdered if she left Lane. But Sarah realized there was something else, something that appears to have been inbred in the women on both sides of her family. That something else was a strange but cogent belief that, no matter how poorly women were treated, their role in the family was to please the men. If they pleased them, the tradition had it, the men would appreciate it and quit beating and abusing the women.

Years later Sarah would realize how stupid and naïve that thought mechanism was. But she knew that her mother, her grandmother, her great-grandmother, and other women going back generations practiced that convoluted domestic theory and suffered hideously for it. At the time she was the target of Lane's outbursts of violence, Sarah was under the foolish impression that the beatings and the abuse were, perhaps, partly her fault and that if she could somehow find a way to please his worship, his behavior toward her would change magically.

In those desperate moments after a thrashing or more "stupid bitch, goddam whore" epithets, she found herself sobbing and mumbling to herself: "If I'm a little bit nicer...if I just improve a bit more, he'll change and won't treat me that way. All I have to do is do what he wants me to do, and he'll be kind to me." And that, of course, was part of her problem throughout the ten years she remained with Lane. It was like waiting to be escorted to Hell itself.

In the meantime, his language grew coarser by the day. He no longer had any inhibitions where Sarah was concerned and no reason to lull her with kind words and promises of better things to come. He had an enormous library full of books she didn't believe he had read. In the decade she worked in his firm, she never saw him reading a book from his library. But that didn't keep him from forcing others to read them. He would give her four or five books on financial planning or some aspect of managing one's own resources and say:

"I want you to read these books in the next week and give me a rundown on what each one has to say. That's part of your job here, and you'd better not fail."

Failing, she knew by that time, meant more beatings and other emotional abuses, as well. True to his word, he would quiz her a week later on the content of each of the books, and she found, to her great relief, that he accepted her versions of what the authors said. Now she knew what she had only suspected in the beginning: He accepted her reports without question because he had not read the books himself and did not want to disclose that fact by engaging her in a discussion of them. His demand that she read and assimilate four or five books a week went on for at least the first five years she worked at the management firm.

In a way, he did her a tremendous favor, a favor he hadn't intended. The books gave her an education in all aspects of financial planning, management, business administration, retirement and benefit programs, and estate planning. It was the career education she had desired and could not have—and now she owed that "favor" to a brute. What a peculiar turnabout those books were to engineer! In effect, she came to know more about Lane's business operation than he did.

Soon she was running the business, and with his approval, because it meant he would have more time for his philandering and his secret trips to gambling resorts. She took over the recruiting of new clients for the financial planning sessions and the maintenance of business relations with new and repeat clients. More and more, Lane had to send her on trips to the East and the South to interview prospective clients or to solidify planning programs other clients had already undertaken.

The trips were a blessing for her, because they meant several days of freedom from his emotional abuse, his beatings, and the obligatory rapes, all of which resumed when she returned. The relationship was still hellish, but now she felt she was slowly turning the tables on this miserable Svengali and would some day be able to repay him for the years of torture.

Despite her new-found clout in running the company, he didn't pass up opportunities to show her who was still boss. He not only took special pains at times to mention Mort the Assassin and to add a knowing look that needed no translation; he also took to approaching her with a pistol, particularly when he said she had goofed on something or other or had not brought in a new customer or held on to an old one. He would cock the weapon and put it to her head.

She never knew whether the pistol was loaded, but he would prolong the agony by cussing her out at the top of his voice and then pulling the trigger. It was a cruel, agonizing version of Russian roulette not even the Russians had considered.

The soothing trips she made alone and away from Lane were more than offset by the bombastic, turbulent trips she was forced to make with him. She had done so well in recruiting more clients that the firm had to employ another person for secretarial and other office duties. She was a former schoolteacher named Karen, and it was clear from the outset that she would not be one to tolerate any of Lane's advances or abuse. However, her presence meant he could no longer use the office bedroom for his sexual games and that he would have to find another means of getting Sarah alone.

His way of doing so was to force her to accompany him on quick one-day trips to Portland, Oregon. He arranged them every other week on the pretense that he had business there.

Each time they drove off, her body would turn off and her mind would steel itself for what was coming by retreating to God knows where. They always stayed at the Red Lion Inn in Portland, and they always had a large rum drink for starters. That is, she did, alone. He was still faking his. She had learned to hate rum, but she forced it down, and at least two or three more, to render herself immune from the rapes he called lovemaking.

On each occasion, she was responsible for reserving their rooms, making sure they were adjoining, and God forbid if they weren't. She also had to see to the drinks, the hors d'oevres, and dinner. It was like arranging the details for her own funeral. Invariably, he insisted when they arrived that she had screwed up in one detail or another. It was his way of introducing another diatribe against her and either the threat of another beating or going through with the beating itself. His line, as usual, followed the now familiar pattern:

"Incompetent fucking bitch....! You don't do anything right....! What are you going to do about it...?" Etc, ad infinitum.

Then, after he had had his fill of sex, he would turn on the charm like the monstrous hypocrite he was and say, sweetly:

"Let's go have a nice dinner now, shall we?"

That was Lane. He would shift gears in an instant, depending upon his immediate needs. Jekyll and Hyde. The trouble was that he was Mr. Hyde most of the time.

After dinner they always drove somewhere to see a movie. Whenever she stepped into the car, it seemed that was the cue for him to belittle her and to find yet another reason for him to remind her that she was nothing more than "a bitch and a whore." It was always the same routine. Drive to Portland, stay at the same motel, order the same services, perform the same rape routine with her failing or refusing to respond, go to the same restaurant, drive to the same movie theater, return to the motel at the same time, and go through the rape routine one or more times.

In time, he developed a hideous routine he forced her to endure before the inevitable rape. After the usual abuse in the car on the way back to the motel, he would grab her by the neck, look her in the eye, and say, like a madman:

"OK, I want you to go in and take a shower, and I want your body to be red—so red that I can see it red. And if it isn't red, I'll make sure your body is red."

She always had to be crystal clean, spic and span for him. And if she resisted, another severe beating would result. Or he would force her back into the shower, turn on the hot water to the highest degree, and hold her there for minutes, despite her screams. She could never stand extra-hot water, and after her experiences with him, she developed an innate fear of steaming water, even though her senses would leave her body at the slightest indication of pain.

Lane's appetite for sex was insatiable, and he was like a bull. Little wonder that she was turned off on those all-night sessions and never reciprocated nor had an orgasm. It was her body's way of repulsing the deranged bull. He demanded that she take frequent ultra-hot showers, yet he never took one himself.

When they left the motel in the morning, he would have her "go and muss up" her bed to make it appear that she had slept in it and also "dirty the towels" so the chambermaid wouldn't suspect a thing. Sarah wondered why he was so concerned about what a chambermaid would think.

Once, in an effort to wound her, he told her with a sneer that he had slept with hundreds of whores "and every one of them was a far better lay than you are."

His boast about his sexual prowess was instantly believable. On more than one occasion at the office, she had blundered into his office on business and found that she had interrupted a petting session he was having with one of the women he called in as a "consultant."

Sarah would say something like, "Oh, excuse me. I didn't know you were busy." And he would turn red and yell at her: "Get the hell out of here! I told you I don't want to be interrupted!"

No, indeed. He hated such "interruptions." She'd try to tell him there was an extremely important phone call for him, but he would say: "I don't give a damn! Just get out!"

At least one of those office relationships developed into more than a sometime thing. She was an interior designer who had become pregnant. Sarah never found out if he was the father, but he gave her a car and also ordered Sarah to deliver a check for $2,000, a large bouquet of flowers, and a dozen balloons to her when she had the baby. That relationship went on for some time, and there were others, too.

Did his wife know about the check and the baby and two or three of the other romantic escapades? Sarah believed she knew about all of them and went on pretending they never happened. Some marriage that was.

CHAPTER 7

Again and again, Sarah asked herself why she continued living in a hell that was not of her own making.

In retrospect, she was amazed by her naïve attitude in the years she spent with Lane's company. Despite the beatings, the mental punishment, and the emotional harassment, she refused to give up the notion that she herself was mainly at fault. In the foolish tradition she had absorbed from generations in her family, she continued to reason that if she were "a little bit nicer and did her job better, then he'll be nice to me." Obviously she was in a trance—a trance that lasted nearly ten years.

One of the reasons she kept returning to and relying on that ridiculous notion was that there were occasional periods in which Lane and others in the family actually treated her like a human being—for whatever ulterior motive suited them. And they gave her hope that, somehow, things would change. Could it be that she'd been wrong in her judgment and that she'd deserved the oral and physical beatings?

Early on, shortly after her divorce from David became final, her health deteriorated from the long hours she was devoting to the job, the harassment she had had to endure, and a strange loss of appetite. She began to lose weight and was so weak she couldn't keep up with the work at the office. In that condition, she became very hostile and snapped at everyone. At first, Lane was furious and threatened to fire her. If only he had!

But when he and his wife Darlene saw how serious her condition had become, they realized something had to be done. They took her to a naturopath, who determined her blood-sugar count had deteriorated and that she was either hypoglycemic or a borderline diabetic—or its opposite. He started her on the five-hour glucose-tolerance test, which requires sampling blood at intervals after drinking a liquid. She never got through it. After the first sampling, she returned to the office just a couple blocks away to do a little work before the next sampling. She went into a comatose state as her blood sugar overloaded, and she needed immediate medical help.

Doctor's orders were to eat regularly, eliminate sugar and sugar-producing foods, exercise daily, and take prescribed supplements. Lane and Darlene were helpful then. Besides making sure she had medical attention and followed orders, they told her to stay away from the office for a couple weeks. The diet, the medicine, and the exercise worked. But, most important, Sarah had the feeling that Lane & Co. did care for her at last and was interested in her well-being. In two weeks, she returned to the office, rested and rejuvenated, and expected to begin a new existence there.

The bubble burst within the first few minutes. Lane behaved as if she had never been gone. As surly and foul-mouthed as ever, he berated her for letting the office go to hell and for foulups she had not had a chance to commit. All was as unpleasant as it had been before, and her spirits dropped. At least her health was repaired and she knew what she had to do to stay that way.

In time, she realized she had become invaluable to the company, even though no one would acknowledge it. Her efforts alone were responsible for bringing in many professional clients for consultations, advice on how to manage their business and personal affairs, and how to increase their incomes. But she remained uneasy doing it, because she felt—no, she *knew*—Lane was gouging them for the services he and Sarah rendered. Most of them were dentists who were having trouble maintaining their practice or realizing the profits they thought they should have been receiving. They would come in for two or three days of conferences, staying at a condo Lane owned for the purpose. And for the few days of interviews and conferences, he would send them bills for anywhere from $50,000 to $75,000! It was outrageous. Whenever she protested that the bloated fees were making it harder and harder to attract new clients, her reward was either another beating or a verbal lashing featuring the foulest four-letter words. Or both.

Many of the clients seemed satisfied, because they experienced some improvement in their practice or business after the consultations. But, then, few had ever had such associations, and they thought the exorbitant fee was the only way to achieve even a slight improvement in their financial status. A few years down the road and a short time before Sarah finally left the company, the rumblings began over the high fees, and the complaints started coming in earnest. So did the lawsuits.

Earlier, when she was at her peak in recruiting and clearly a major asset to the company, Lane and Darlene made a curious request. Her mother wasn't speaking to her and her ex-husband and brother and sisters had blocked her out of their lives. As a result, she had no one she could call family or friend to lean on or listen to her woes or even her successes as a businesswoman. Would she, Lane and Darlene asked, consent to be adopted as their legal daughter and thereby have them become her new family?

She must have been out of her mind to consider it, but she did. With twisted logic, she reasoned: "Nobody else wants me; maybe this would mean the end of the beatings, the mental and emotional harassment, and, finally, an acknowledgement that I am an important cog in the operation of the financial-management firm. I'm 30 and life may be quickly passing me by. What can I lose?'"

As macabre as it was, they went through the process of a legal, adult adoption. If only Sarah had read the fine print! Not till it was too late did she realize that her new adoptive status forbid her to have any contact with her mother or Mom's new husband, her stepfather. It also meant that she was now imprisoned within Lane's nest egg and that she might never be able to get out, unless he chose to get rid of her. She was trapped legally. It was one of the greatest mistakes she had made.

But it also led to her second serious mistake. Soon afterward, at a time when she was at her peak as the company's sales representative, Lane suggested that she would be even more successful in recruiting clients if she could carry the title of "President" of the company! Sarah, still in a stupor, was impressed. Was he serious? It was a joke, wasn't it? Both Lane and Darlene assured her it was no joke, that she had earned the title, and that her monthly pay would be increased, as well. It also meant that she would, in effect, "own" the company! Or so she was led to believe.

Sarah was ecstatic, believing she had made it, at last. Lane told her it would be a great experience to be the owner of her own company and that she had earned it. Her thoughts at the time were:

"Here I am, a single woman, with no college education and only a high-school diploma. Born and reared in virtual poverty. Product of a violent, dysfunctional family. And now I am taking over and operating a company with an annual profit of more than a million dollars! Look what I've done!"

In a few years, she would learn how she had been duped into becoming the "fall guy" for the company's indiscretions. But at that moment and for the year or so, she would behave in a different way. Armed with the new title and better pay, she became a hardened business woman, who now had a very personal reason for luring new clients into the fold.

Her demeanor became calculating and her sales pitch brash. Some saw through her new approach, but many more were impressed with her "business-like" technique and bold line. Those that got away were the lucky ones. Those that didn't and signed contracts for $50,000 to $70,000 realized that she was there strictly on business and that she was going to get their money in return for promises that they would make more.

Those promises, canceled out by Lane's incompetence, would cause her to reflect: "The customers who paid the price are on my conscience and represent my biggest regret. I am ashamed of the 'snow job' I leveled at clients, many of whom were in dangerous financial condition and could go broke if our advice didn't rescue them—as it often failed to do."

In the meantime, Lane, now armed with legal papers making Sarah his adopted daughter and the president of the company he swiftly placed in her name, had all he needed to assume full control of her life. He had his name on all her checking accounts and credit cards, and he also owned whatever car she drove, registering it under the corporation's name, but requiring her to make the payments and pay for maintenance. Even the house she bought was 50 percent his. There wasn't anything she could do without his knowledge or approval. Although she was the mainstay of the company, she was receiving only $2,000 a month in salary—out of which she had to pay mortgage fees, the property tax, the home insurance, and all other expenses for the house and the car.

His taunt at the time was, "After all, I'm paying you a salary and you're not worth it. Why in hell should you complain? You've got it easy!"

It didn't matter to him that she was working 100 hours a week and was at his beck and call seven days and seven nights a week. A whore, she observed, makes much more than $2,000 a month and doesn't have to take the punishment she had to absorb.

So, why didn't she pack up and leave? Where could she go? She had no family nor even a support group to listen to her troubles. As horrible as her situation was, she at least had her own home. She had a roof over her head, as the saying goes. She had a job and regular pay, adequate clothing, and a car.

For all those niceties, she paid a terrible price. She had sold her soul to the devil. But isn't that what a great many women do every day of their lives? Their appearance to the world is more important than how they appear to themselves. An honest look in the mirror is what they sacrifice, and most women don't realize it's the most important thing they possess.

Maturity came late to Sarah Summers. It had taken her a long time to learn that women grow up in a society that insists they are placed on earth to please others, not themselves. When she thought back on her turbulent childhood, she realized that no importance was given to what she had learned in her studies. She was a prolific reader and loved school, but only Grandma Summers recognized it and appealed to her thirst for learning and beauty. Her parents were far too busy or absent to care. She started piano lessons at 9 and made rapid progress in the two years before she left Lethbridge. It could have been the bridge to a much better future, but when she fled Canada, her dream of becoming a performer at the keyboard fled with it. If she could have stayed behind with Grandma Summers, her story would have been far different—and undoubtedly so much happier that it need not ever have been committed to paper.

Sarah met many women whose early years were like hers. It didn't matter what dreams they might have had, what talents they possessed that were waiting to be cultivated, what inner needs they harbored. What mattered was how much they pleased others, mostly men.

She and other women were born and bred primarily to breed. Most men look at them that way, despite the increasing political clout of the women's movement. Women are simply hired hands whose reason for being is to keep house and home in order, to run the kitchen, and to look delectable in the bedroom.

It was easy to fall into the prescribed mold. Sarah was looked upon as a professional woman when she was under Lane's Rasputin-like spell, and she was dressed up to look like one and expected to act like one. He selected all her clothes for her, from underwear to coat. When she bought clothing, he demanded that she take it home so he could inspect it. He determined the length of the skirts she wore and the height of the heels on every new pair of shoes. She was not permitted to buy or wear an open-toed shoe or the back-strapped type.

Sarah was restricted to navy blue, black, or bone colors; no other. If she dared show up in the office with anything he had not approved or which didn't meet his rigid specifications, he would send her home to change after the predictable oral and physical assaults.

Lane also dictated her hairstyle, despite the fact that she had had experience as a hairdresser and obviously knew much more about women's hairstyles than he did. She had preferred wearing her hair short, but that wasn't good enough for him. Once, after returning from the hairdresser's, he looked at her hair and said, grumpily:

"Not short enough. Go back and get it cut shorter."

She had no choice. It was either do as he ordered or suffer the inevitable beating and oral lashing.

He controlled the type of makeup she wore, which was so light that she may as well not have been wearing any at all. Lipstick was a definite no-no. He was adamantly opposed to her wearing anything that made her look feminine. Consequently, her wardrobe for the office consisted mainly of navy blue, black, or soft-tweed suits. One of the reasons she looked forward eagerly to business trips was that she could wear what she wished and behave normally.

Was he jealous?

The more accurate term was "possessive." He didn't want anyone to see her as a sex object. His purpose was to take all the femininity out of her, except when he held her captive in his bedroom. Her shirts and blouses always had to be half way up the neck. She never wore anything with a V-neck. Everything had to be long-sleeved and cuffed at the wrist. Everything had to be covered up. She would have been at home in some of the heavily restricted, male-controlled countries of the Middle East. In order to make sure that her nipples would not show through, he supervised the purchase of all her bras—as well as the rest of her underwear!

In the summer she was not permitted to wear shorts or a tank top, and if she wanted to wear a T-shirt, it could not be tight to the body; it had to be loose-fitting. Ironically, she paid all the bills for everything she wore or possessed out of the meager paycheck she received.

Like a modern version of Hitler's SS, he would go to her house at least once a week to examine the premises. One of his targets was her reading matter. She wasn't permitted to read anything that wasn't business-related. No magazines. No "trash," as he called it.

"If you have enough luxury time to sit around reading junk or watching TV, you'd better use it learning something from a good book on financial management."

If Sarah had any reading matter she knew wouldn't meet his "requirements," she always kept it out of sight, under mattresses or covered up in bureau or desk drawers, because he had a habit of dropping in without calling first. Among the "forbidden" reading matter were several religious books, which she read in those days to keep her sanity. If he caught her reading them, it would have meant another beating.

In the relatively few hours that she managed to be out of Lane's clutches, she permitted herself one great indulgence—ballet lessons. She had always loved ballet and decided she would take the lessons when he would not miss her at the office or at home. It gave her another wonderful breather away from him. However, he saw her one day from a distance as she was getting into her car. She was wearing her dance outfit, which included a tight T-shirt that was flesh-colored. He didn't think she was wearing anything on top. The next day at work he beat her even more severely than usual and pinned her against the wall, his hands around her throat, as if he intended choking her to death. He wanted her to quit going to the ballet school, but she vowed only to be more careful and cover herself up whenever she left for the evening classes.

The crowning insult was Lane's purchase of a wedding ring he forced her to wear at all times. He didn't want anyone to think she was a single woman and available! What reason did he give her for wearing the ring?

"It would be a very negative message to clients, Sarah, if they thought you were single, and it might turn off the wives of clients. The men might consider 'picking you up' if they got the idea that you were unattached and available."

She knew he had flipped his lid, but she realized the path of least resistance and less abuse was to concede he had a point. But she never wore the ring when she was out of his sight.

Whatever else she thought of him, she had to admit he was extremely clever in keeping his violent behavior toward her from the eyes and ears of others. In the presence of others, he treated her like the woman she dreamed of being. But when they were alone, the beast emerged, like a monster out of science-fiction. When she awoke each morning, she fantasized that she had only dreamed of being beaten and emotionally harassed, but when she saw the bruises on her body, she knew the nightmare was reality.

Everything in her life was dictated by him—except her periods. She thanked God he couldn't control them. When she told him one had started, he would get upset and launch another oral assault against her. Early on, she began lying to him about frequent periods to avert the incessant rapes as best she could. But later on, in the last and worst year of her association with him, she no longer had to lie. Her body let her down again, and she began having periods nearly every week. Something was terribly wrong, and this time she refused to have Lane and Darlene pick one of their ersatz medicine men for her. She sought out her own doctor, who put her through extensive tests and diagnosed her condition as severe "clinical depression." This illness would not go away as quickly as the others had.

CHAPTER 8

Despite her success in broadening the company's income base, Lane's attitude toward Sarah didn't improve. In fact, he became more brutal than ever. If she didn't bring home the bacon each time out and nail down another $70,000 fee, he was more scurrilous than ever and seemed to put even more muscle into the beatings he gave her.

It gradually dawned on her after reading the fine print in the documents she had unwittingly signed that the main reason for his renewed belligerence resided in those documents. They bound her in slavery and made her liable for whatever pitfalls lay ahead. And there was always the threat of Mort, if those didn't do the trick.

She was president of a financial-management company and drawing less than $30,000 a year. But that was only a part of her life as a slave. She had to eat every meal with Lane and his family, seven days and seven nights each week. The hours she kept, the frequent traveling, and the responsibility of overseeing new and old contracts were rough on her health. She weighed barely more than 100 pounds in those years and wore clothing that ranged between Sizes 2 and 4. Her scarecrow visage looked all the more bizarre because it was distributed over a body that was 5 feet 7.

As if her physical problems weren't enough to bear, Lane decided to sell the home-style office they had been working in and expand operations. He opened a suite of offices in a nearby building and chose a hillside mansion in need of remodeling for his new home. The mansion had a pool and a separate building that would be used as his office and library, as well as for conferences with prospective clients.

Mansion or no, she had to move into a much larger house just across the street. Again, how convenient. This time her situation grew uglier than ever. In the three or four months prior to moving the business office and staff into the new building, she had to work out of Lane's back office, the building separated from the home. Now she had to put up with his beatings and abuse at any time during the 20-hour work days.

The years she served as president of the company were a combination of hell and heaven—hell when she was anywhere near Lane, which was most of the time, and heaven when she could get out on the road away from him, meet some decent people, and offer them financial help they desperately needed, despite the exorbitant fees Lane imposed. She dreaded the end of an assignment in another city, because it meant repeating the dreaded ritual of the trip home and what awaited her there.

As it had to, the collapse of the company began in her last year there. One day, Lane, triggered by another of his tyrannical outbursts, administered one of his worst beatings. It was accompanied by a threat she had heard so often ("I ought to kill you right here and now so that we would both be better off!"). This time he had an additional surprise for her. He shouted that she had "screwed up so badly that I'm going to hire somebody else to run the company." Then, as he had done so often, he said he thought it was time he made a call to his old friend, Mort the Assassin, and Sarah winced again. She had made mistakes now and then, but this time she had done absolutely nothing wrong. It was simply that he had to do his thing in a violent way to satisfy his ego and divert blame from himself. And also to keep her in line.

Within the week, Lila Desmond arrived to take over the firm, subject to Lane's wishes and desires, of course. And Sarah was relegated to the sales position she had always had, but this time without the prestige of the "presidency," by now a thoroughly hollow-sounding sobriquet. Lila was an experienced financial manager with many years of top-level experience, and she was several years older than Sarah. But more important, because Sarah was certain it was the main reason Lane hired her, she was an attractive blonde with a slim figure.

At first, Lila and Sarah became friends, mainly because Sarah indicated she bore no grudge against Lila for taking over her job. In fact, Lila seemed sympathetic to Sarah at first and went to her defense on a couple of occasions when Lane castigated Sarah at board meetings. It was the first time anyone in the inner circle had taken up Sarah's cause and spoken for her, and it worked for a while.

In that brief period, Lane withheld his abuse and didn't lay a hand on Sarah. Also in that brief period, Lila indicated to Sarah that she and Lane had once had a "relationship." After that revelation, Sarah quit confiding in her, realizing she'd be foolhardy to trust her. Sarah soon discovered Lila was something of a double agent and prodded her for intimate information she could pass on to Lane.

When the beatings and abuse began once again, Sarah knew that the "friend" she thought she had found was anything but that. At board meetings, Sarah became so defiant that she surprised herself. What the hell, she thought, she was going to take a beating anyway, so she may as well say what she really thought. Lane would say nothing during the meeting, but afterward he'd find Sarah alone and rave:

"How can you embarrass me like that in front of people! You paid me no respect! You don't know how important it is to run this company!"

Who gave a damn? Sarah wasn't running the company any more, and if she were to suffer still another beating for mistakes others made, she would be able at least to claim a moral victory for having said her piece.

Lane was like a well-trained pup around Lila. She always got her way with him and ran the company as she wished. Sarah was suspicious. She wondered what Lila had on him that turned him into a whimpering servant in her presence. She ruled the roost—but it was too late for Lane, the company, and his family.

In the middle of Sarah's last year with the firm, the bubble burst. It came during and after a most disappointing business trip, during which she had produced no potential income, because the word was now out that Lane and the company were "gyp artists" and that their advice was not only worthless but dangerous. Sarah collapsed from exhaustion and required medical attention while on the trip.

On her return to Seattle, Lane unleashed his worst assault on her, physically and orally. She collapsed again and had to be taken to the hospital for treatment and tests. Her doctor's verdict was that she seemed to have suffered a slight stroke on the road and was now in a state of "clinical depression." The combination of a disastrous business trip with Lane's bombastic abuse, the doctor indicated, had put her under intolerable stress.

Once more the thought of suicide invaded Sarah's mind, and once more she managed to fight it off. Through it all, she thought: "How in hell could I be reacting this way physically when my body automatically shuts itself off whenever violence and pain threaten me?'"

The day after she returned home from a week's stay in the hospital, Lane called and in an angry voice shouted: "Get over here right now! I'll give you five minutes! If you don't, I'll come over to get you—or make a phone call to Mort!"

When she entered the office, still groggy from the illness, the room was dark, as usual. He was standing by his desk, like a sinister shadow from a bad horror movie. In two steps, he was by her side and grabbed her, one arm around her neck and the other holding a revolver.

"I think I'll end all this crap right now and blow your fucking brains out! You're nothing but a worthless piece of shit anyway!"

At that moment, Sarah didn't give a damn what he did. He could have saved her the trouble of going through with suicide. With what little voice she could manage through his stranglehold on her neck, she said:

"Then go ahead and do it, goddam it! Put me out of my misery and get me rid of you, at last! You make me so fucking sick I can't stand it any more."

Her words surprised her. But, there, she had finally said what had been on her lips more than nine years. He could see that she was at the end of her rope and that she was nearly insane.

Lane suddenly let her go and in a much softer voice said: "Why don't you go on back home and indulge in a little more self-pity. G'wan. Go home and lie on your bed and cry!"

For the next two days, she contemplated going out to buy a gun and ending his life before he ended hers. But the thought of going to prison for murder just for eliminating a scum of a man soothed the fire in her belly and helped bring about a strange peace she had not known before—a peace growing out of the recognition that she was about to put an end to ten years of horror.

She didn't leave Lane and the firm immediately, because she had many loose ends to tie down, but she knew she would be gone soon. Totally disgusted and demoralized, she stopped any pretense at selling and soon discovered that without her sales, the company was doomed. Nobody else was selling either, nor had they been doing so for many months. Now she understood at last that the company would have folded years earlier if it had not been for her efforts at day-and-night selling. She had within her own grasp a sure-fire weapon to use against Lane all that time and didn't know it!

At almost the same time, the lawsuits began appearing. Sarah wondered what had taken them so long. Most of them were legal complaints that the fees were way too high for the advice given. In some of the cases, the clients also charged that the advice from Lane was so far off base that their practice or business went into the red or was forced into bankruptcy. Lane's attorney managed to quash a few of the suits, but the force of numbers meant his financial-management firm was headed for the dustbin. Greed had finally been its own reward.

Sarah had mixed feelings when she saw the end approach. The many clients she had recruited and learned to know so well were like a family to her—the family she felt she had never had. When she had first met them, they were simply clients who had to listen to her rehearsed sales pitch. But when they poured out their tales of woe and their need for help to avert financial ruin or bankruptcy, her attitude softened and they became friends. They looked to her to find a way to get them out of a hole, and she suffered along with them, knowing all the time that Lane's outlandish fees and questionable advice would ultimately be their reward. She knew that he would not take care of them, but she did and realized she had to. They would call her at work, at home, or wherever they could get her to relate their latest worries, because she was a friend they felt they could trust.

If only Lane had felt the same way. While she became interested in their well-being and their success in business and at home, he was interested only in their money. She never tried to keep anything from him. She didn't dare. At work he had all company phone lines available to him at his desk, and he would listen in on her conversations whenever he saw her extension light up. Big Brother was always watching and listening. It was one of the many reasons she felt like an escapee when she met the clients on the road at their homes or places of business.

Among the clients she remembered best were a young and very attractive Jewish couple, David and Karen, from the South. He was a children's dentist, who found himself in a rut in his practice, a rut that was also affecting his marriage adversely. Sarah spent a great deal of time with them, at their home and at his dental office, and eventually brought them with her to the Seattle office for consultations. When they returned home, they reorganized both the dental practice and their home life. In a year and a half, David had tripled his practice, and it appeared that he had saved his marriage, too. At least for a time.

Sarah visited him months later, and he insisted on taking her to dinner to talk about his now flourishing practice. But he also talked about his domestic life, which was still having some problems. When he began telling her how much she looked like his sister, whom he loved dearly, she began to feel uncomfortable. In a moment she knew why.

Near the end of the dinner, he put a hand on hers and said: "If I were to leave Karen, would you consider....?"

"No, no! Absolutely not!" Sarah almost shouted it out, not letting him finish. Although she was flattered by the question, she was totally unprepared for its intent. That was the last time she permitted herself to be alone with him or, in fact, to have personal contact with David and Karen. It would have been easy to say "Yes" to what was undoubtedly an offer of a one-night stand, not marriage. But the mechanisms that had built up inside her in a lifetime of abuse, violence, and the fear of pain, caused her mouth to cry "No!" before her mind ordered it.

Since most of her clients were dentists, Sarah had also come to know that domestic problems and divorce run through the dental community.

She was sure it had a lot to do with the training and the profession itself. Dentistry, by its very nature, she had observed, was a hostile profession, very hostile. They do things to people that people don't want done. People go to them because they have to be there, not because they want to be there. It's painful. And dentists are employing all kinds of different gases and chemicals that affect the psyche of the patient.

Sarah knew her opinion would be contradicted, but her wide experience with hundreds of dentists convinced her: She had not met one dentist she could call a truly happy person. For reasons she believed only a psychiatrist could discern, the largest problem plaguing dentists and their wives was psychological, although personal and professional hurdles played an important role. Most of the younger dentists she met seemed to have little or no self-esteem. She emphasized the "younger" qualification. The number of consultants in dentistry is far greater than the number in medicine. Her quick calculation was three consultants to every dentist in the U.S. Sarah found nothing like it in medicine or other professions.

Why was that the case with dentists? First, she surmised, it had something to do with the way they were reared as children and, second, it was related to the culture from which they emerged. Her observation was that dentists most often spring from a blue-collar culture. Contrast that with their brothers and sisters in medicine. Dentists' fathers are usually laborers of some sort, while medical doctors usually have parents who are professional or business people or are entrepreneurs. In other words, they're the kind of people who are not afraid to take risks. Dentists rarely come from that kind of an environment.

In addition to all that, Sarah compared the way dentists and medical doctors are trained. Almost directly opposite in nature. Dentists are "torn down" in the colleges and universities. They go through hell to get that degree and start their practice. Talk to your dentist; if he's honest, he'll tell you he knew that if he could survive the training, he'd make it in dentistry. For example, they are made to buy all their required tools and equipment the very first year, so that if they want to drop out of dental school the second year they'll already be a thousand bucks or so in debt. So they think twice about withdrawing.

Sarah was convinced Lane concentrated on dentists as clients because they were so vulnerable and easy for him to manipulate— and to charge his outlandish fees. He could also control them in his consultation sessions, whereas doctors or lawyers would walk away from him when they learned what they would receive in return for the sky-high charges.

In one of Lane's most serious disagreements, a longtime client, Vernon Danton, charged Lane and the company with destroying his dental practice, forcing him into bankruptcy, and breaking up his marriage in the process. After Lane and his attorney wrote a letter to Danton, the dentist decided not to press his case. Sarah suspected he did so because Lane threatened in the letter that if the dentist persisted and filed a lawsuit, Lane would make public some of the most intimate personal problems Danton had confessed to Lane in consultation sessions.

Sarah believed Danton's troubles were mainly of his own making, but she was convinced that if he wanted to make an unbeatable case against Lane and his attorney, all he had to do was take the letter to the authorities and file a criminal suit. What Lane had done, in effect, was violate one of the most sacred trusts in American life—the sanctity of the personal relationship in medicine, law, or any other profession.

Danton accused Lane of gouging, and he had a legitimate complaint. He had paid out more than $150,000 for consultations in a relatively short period. It would have been no consolation to him, but many other clients had been bled even more. One who should have sued (but didn't), because he had a much stronger case than Danton, was an Arizona dentist who coughed up more than $280,000 in fees before he realized he was being taken for a ride.

In all those years before the clients discovered they were being overcharged shamelessly, all that ill-begotten money went into the pockets of Lane and Darlene, and Sarah was one of the chief victims of their ego and greed. She had come to trust no one, because she feared no one could trust her. It's the lot of a person who has been abused relentlessly over a period of years. At 35 she had retreated even further into herself and she was mortified to realize she had forgotten how to have friends or personal relationships. It would take her a long time to emerge from that self-imposed prison.

CHAPTER 9

The main reason Sarah couldn't walk away from Lane & Co. the day of their worst encounter was that the legal trap he had set for her continued to defy a solution. She had not yet determined how she could break free without serious, lasting damage to herself.

A short time before the final explosion occurred, Lane and Darlene had gone on a trip, ostensibly to spend some leisure time at a sunny resort and talk to an old financial friend, Ralph Jameson, about how to convert their estate to a retirement umbrella. Darlene had inherited at least $6 million from her mother, who had died the year before. Sarah believed she finally knew the reason Lane had not cast her off. Greed, again. But she never fully understood why Darlene, with so much cash coming her way, didn't divorce her bed-hopping, violent husband, who had verbally abused her so often in their strange marriage. She had to believe they were both sick, very sick, and deserved each other.

What Sarah learned a few weeks later was that they had traveled to the resort, all right, but not to gather sunshine, nor simply to "plan their retirement." They had met with Ralph, but Sarah was the main topic of discussion. With so many lawsuits pending and the company rapidly accumulating heavy debts, they needed a scapegoat to be the target of any legal actions that might ensue. And Sarah was to be the scapegoat.

After all, she had served as president of the firm and she was also their "adopted daughter"—all of it in writing and noted on legal documents.

She would be grateful forever to Ralph for what happened next. He listened attentively to everything Lane and Darlene had to say and pretended to be in sympathy with what they intended to do. Their scheme was to set up a new corporation in their name that would be designed to protect them against any liability, any lawsuits that might arise. Under that plan, everything they owned, including their home, cars, furnishings, and all collateral and investments, would be included in the new corporation. Then they would create a second corporation in Sarah's name that would include everything she owned, and it would include the failing company. From their standpoint, everything they projected appeared to be legal and might have been considered to be so by an outsider or even a judge.

Darlene wrote Sarah a letter detailing all they had intended and asking her to go along with the plan, "because it's in your best interests, Dear."

Sarah might have been naïve enough to agree and sign the papers had it not been for Ralph's phone call. He had been a good friend to her before, and he certainly turned out to be a great friend when she needed one most. She had met him a year earlier on a brief vacation trip to Hawaii, her first vacation in ten years. Every morning she was there, she took a walk on the beach and Ralph would be there snorkeling.

They became good friends and discovered they had a lot in common because they were in the same business field. In that short time, they created a pleasant rapport, mainly because he learned what a hectic life she had led and the volatile existence she had endured with Lane, whose temper tantrums and pugnacious behavior he had already known something about. Ralph turned out to be one of the few guardian angels in her life.

Every word of Ralph's phone message was etched in Sarah's memory forever.

"Sarah, I want to warn you about what's in the works for them and for you. What they are prescribing, despite my precautions, may sound legal and legitimate on the surface and a court just might accept it, but don't you believe it. If you sign these papers and agree to their scheme, don't call me again for any help. Agree to their proposition and you'll become liable for thousands, perhaps millions, in damages, and maybe even some jail time. You will be responsible for all the company's debts and for the pending lawsuits. And they'll get off Scot-free behind their legal wall of corporate trusts. I tried to talk them out of their legal plan, but it was useless."

Sarah was shivering with indecision and asked herself myriad questions in a matter of seconds: "How could they make me liable for the company and all their debts? What judge or court would believe that I had been duped not once but many times? How could they escape without penalty and make me the goat?"

Because Ralph was so sincere and urgent, she promised him she would sign nothing without his approval.

"Thanks, Ralph. You're the friend I always thought you were. But how could you pretend to advise them and still tell me not to sign anything they send me?"

"Because, Sarah, I trust you. Now, remember, call me at any time you need me—and, let me repeat, do not sign anything that lets them off the hook. Promise?"

She promised. Almost immediately, she had further proof that his warning was justified. Lane called her, using his most businesslike voice:

"We need $60,000 right away to pay off the company's bills and debts. Pronto! I want you to call Joe DiNardo today and tell him we need $60,000 to buy that piece of property we recommended to him as part of his new retirement plan. He knows all about it and is waiting for my OK. Do not, under any circumstances, tell him why we really need the money. If you do, you're dead meat! Besides, we'll make it good all the way around. All we're bargaining for is a little more time."

What a dilemma! With Ralph's words still ringing in her ears and Lane's threat bringing a shiver down her back, she sat stunned, trying to make a decision. What should she do? After an hour in a scary trance, she made up her mind: She would call DiNardo, tell him what Lane wanted her to tell him, and ask him for his check. Then she would call Ralph again for more instructions. Operating like a robot, Sarah called Joe and asked him to send the money as soon as he could. He offered no resistance, telling her he was waiting for Lane's go-ahead on the real-estate deal.

"Of course, I'm going to need several days, because I'll have to liquidate some stocks to raise the money, but I'll have it in your hands as soon as I can."

Just as she moved back to the phone once again to call Ralph, it rang. Lane was on the line again.

"Did you call Joe?"

"Yes. I told him just what you told me." She wondered if he could detect the terrible trembling in her voice. "Joe sounded happy to know you had arranged for the purchase of the property, and he's putting together the cash and will send the money whenever the stock liquidation is final."

"OK, now get this straight. When you get the money, deposit it in your name and write me a check over your signature for the entire amount. Got it? I'll put a hold on the retirement property right away. That way, as soon as I get a check from you, I'll be able to nail down the deal for Joe. If he delays, he will be missing the opportunity of a lifetime. And if you delay, you'll be sorry. It may be the ideal time to call Mort."

Frantic, Sarah dialed Ralph's number in California and spilled out the details of Lane's call.

"If you do what he asks and then sign a check turning over that amount of cash to Lane, you'll be committing a felony. And if you do that, I want no further discussions with you."

"So what should I do, Ralph?" Sarah was shaking so hard she could barely hang on to the phone.

"Hire an attorney right away and tell him the whole story. Everything. Then call me tomorrow and we'll go from there. Got a pencil? Here, take the names of three good attorneys I know in the Seattle area. One of them may take your case—or refer you to another good attorney who will. Understand?"

She followed his advice, and lucky for her that she did, or she might have been telling her story from a jail cell. The Christmas season was approaching, not the best of times to be calling for legal help, but what else could she do? All three attorneys she called said their case load was bulging and they couldn't take on a new case. But one of them offered her several more names.

The seventh lawyer Sarah called that frenzied day was Fred Roberson, who said he would be away for the holidays but that he would see her in his office if she could get down there that afternoon. She did and, in a three-hour session, told him her story. He sat there mesmerized.

"This is the weirdest, most despicable story of abuse I have ever heard. Please, let me ponder it while I'm away, and I'll let you know when I get back on January 2nd whether I'll take your case. Call me at 7 that morning and I'll tell you what my decision is. In the meantime, I want you to make plans to go into hiding as soon as you are able so you won't continue to be a target for that bully.

Find a safe place and tell no one where you are. Don't use your charge cards or your checks. Gather together as much cash as you may need.

"Oh, and one more thing. I hate to do this to you, but if I take your case, I will need money, a good bit of it, to process the case to and through the courts and, more important, to protect you. You know that no lawyer would be able to do it alone, and it might be a long, hard road for you."

Sarah gulped before answering, but she understood what the stakes were.

"I don't have much in savings, Fred, but I do have a retirement plan that's worth about $50,000, and I could get whatever I need out of that. I don't care what it takes. This is the chance to break free of a curse that has dogged my life, and it's now or never."

Unfortunately, Sarah had to delay her trip to a hiding place for a while, because Lane and Darlene returned from their "vacation" trip. When he learned that Joe's money had not yet been received, he might have administered the beating of Sarah's life had it not been for the presence of Lila, who stepped between them like a referee on Fight Night.

"This hate session has to stop! Now, we're all going to sit down like adults and talk this whole thing out."

She marched a very nervous Sarah, Lane, and Darlene into the meeting room, assigned them seats out of combat range, and sat in the chair reserved for the "chairman," which she was at the moment. Sarah had grown to dislike and distrust her, but she had to admire her for her new role as peacemaker. Lila began:

"I want Sarah to take the next two weeks off, and I don't want her to have any contact with the office. Nor with you, Lane. She's asked for sick leave."

Inwardly, Sarah realized the leave was just what the doctor ordered for her. But Lane couldn't stand it. With a sneer, he said:

"Oh, we're going to take care of pitiful little Sarah again, huh? Poor little overworked Sarah, who can't do anything right. What did she do this time, Lila? She just wants to tell how terrible I've been to her and what an awful life she's had, eh?"

Lila shushed him. And he shushed, temporarily. The questions returned in Sarah's mind: What was the strange power Lila had over this monster? And why is his wife so silent about his escapades and his beastly temper?

Sarah kept saying to herself what she had rehearsed moments before: "Don't say a word, Sarah, no matter what. Anything you say will only make the situation worse."

Lila was laying down the law.

"Absolutely no contact with Sarah, Lane. None. No phone calls. No notes. Nothing. And you're not to go over to her house either. Never. I know the holidays are coming up, but you're to leave her alone for at least two weeks."

Darlene had a voice, at last.

"But what about Christmas? You know, we're a family, and we always have celebrated together."

Some family, Sarah thought. People in jail cells have more compassionate families.

Lane could hold it in no longer.

"Yeah, that's right, Sarah. Run away. You're just good for shit! G'wan, get out of here! Who gives a crap about you anyway?"

His words meant nothing to Sarah any more. She didn't care what he said or thought. Let him kill her or have her killed. It mattered no longer. She was numb to words, to looks, to threats. Her inner voice kept repeating: "I just don't give a goddam what happens to all the people in this room."

Without saying another word, Sarah left the room and went home. There another dilemma awaited her. The $60,000 check from Joe had arrived, addressed to her. Fred Roberson had told her to call him when it came, but when she called his law office, she learned he had just left for the holidays. She put the check in a dresser drawer and covered it with all the hose and panties available, as if hiding it would make it go away.

Darlene called her every hour to ask if she had received the check from Joe. Obviously she had been prodded by Lane to keep calling Sarah. He himself preferred to call her in the middle of the night to tell her what a "no good, useless whore" she was but never mentioning the check from Joe. She hung up on him each time as soon as the cussing began.

Sarah knew she had to put off her escape to a hiding place to just the right time, so she pretended to be interested in the Christmas season. Darlene asked her to join her sister and others in the family for Christmas dinner, as she had each of the previous nine years. She promised that Lane would not be there, in keeping with the gospel according to Lila. Under that condition, Sarah suggested that they permit her to cook and serve the dinner at her place instead, and they agreed. All went reasonably well through the dinner and they opened presents immediately afterward, as they had done the previous nine years. But there was an uneasiness in everyone throughout the evening. For Sarah, it was a prison party in which she was like "the condemned man who ate a hearty meal."

At about 9, when the party was about to break up, in strolled the unwanted and uninvited guest, Lane, who quickly offered a cheerful "Merry Christmas" to all hands, except Sarah. To her, he leaned over and whispered, "Bitch!" Darlene got up to leave. At that moment, he grabbed Sarah by the arm and shoved her into the kitchen.

"I want you to know, you miserable son of a bitch, that you're not going to get away with any of this shit!"

"Get your bloody hands off me! What in hell are you talking about?"

"This escapade of yours. You're so sick you smell like death warmed over. I just want you to know that you're not going to get away with it. You just wait...."

From the other room, Darlene said to him: "We'd better go."

He said to her, sweetly: "OK, Honey, I'll be there in just a minute." The devil himself couldn't have done it better.

In return for her hosting the dinner, Darlene's family asked Sarah to return the favor and join them for dinner at their house the next day. Damn! Another day's delay in her escape to a hiding place! She wanted to refuse, but she couldn't, because she was afraid of tipping off her plan to vanish. Any suspicious moves or words at this point could upset everything.

In the meantime, a heavy snow began to fall, giving Seattle one of its rare white Christmases. Because she had the only four-wheel drive, Sarah was asked to do the driving. She agreed, even though it meant Lane would be going along, too.

That dinner went along reasonably well, too, although once again everyone seemed to be walking on eggs for the explosion that didn't come—until they returned home. Sarah had a habit of backing her car into the garage, which she did. Lane was out of the car first, followed by the others. As she opened the car door to leave, Lane came around to the driver's side. She had reached out to the ground with her left leg when he seized the handle and slammed the door on her ankle. It happened too quickly for her body to steel itself against pain. She screamed and he slammed the door again.

"Bitch! This is an idea of what it's going to be like, and don't you forget it."

Sarah crawled into the house as Lane and Darlene walked across the street to their home. Two minutes later, as Sarah walked to the bathroom to bathe her bloodied and crushed ankle, the phone rang. She should have let it ring. It was his voice again.

"You've made this the worst Christmas of my whole life by the way you've misbehaved, you miserable whore, and I want to tell you that you are never, ever going to do this again to this family."

If she had had reservations in the past about speaking out, they vanished now. The excruciating pain from her messy ankle spurred her on.

"Lane, this is the last conversation you and I will ever have. If you call me one more time, I will first call Lila and then the police. You promised that you would not contact me or bother me in any way. I repeat, you son of a bitch, that I will never talk to you again." And it was her last conversation with him. Free at last!

Her ankle wasn't broken, but X-Rays the next day indicated substantial interior damage to it. She would have to limp and drag it along for several weeks.

The next day she called Ralph in California to tell him about her predicament, the check from Joe, and the fact that her attorney would not return until January 2nd. He didn't hesitate.

"Sarah, I want to repeat this so you will understand. If you cash that check from Joe and handle it under your name, I'll have to have you arrested, because now that you've told me something I know is a felony, I'm equally responsible and subject to prosecution."

It wasn't difficult to go into hiding, as Fred had suggested. She knew why he had advised it and what the consequences might be if she disobeyed. A friend in Olympia agreed to take her in for as long as might be necessary, so she packed what she needed, locked up the house, and before a half hour had passed, she was on her way to her hiding place.

On January 2, she called Fred at 7 in the morning and he told her to meet him in his office in two hours. They spent most of the day arranging her immediate future. Among the legal papers they prepared was a letter to Lane resigning from the company, which she knew was headed for bankruptcy or worse.

She resigned as marketing director and as president of the company, surmising Lane and Darlene had not actually stricken her name as president from the corporate register. She and Fred had guessed right. In time, they discovered Lane and Darlene had not removed her name from the incorporation papers. What more proof did Sarah need that they were setting her up for a gigantic fall so they could protect their fannies?

Fred told her, chuckling, that the ruse would boomerang against Lane and Darlene, because the retention of her name as president would become a negotiating tool on her behalf in any legal battle.

It was a legal battle that was over before it began. The IRS picked up the Lane-Darlene trail, and when Sarah last heard about their predicament, it appeared certain that they were headed for deep trouble with federal investigators over their tax returns. Their problems could be traced back to their decision to remodel their Seattle mansion at great cost.

Sarah has an extremely bitter recollection of that event. When Lane had embarked on the monumental remodeling a few years before, he had grabbed her by the throat, pinned her up against a wall, and snarled:

"If you ever talk to the IRS or anyone else about any of these financial dealings on the house, I'll have you taken care of. I still have Mort's phone number."

Until that moment, she had not been overly fond of the IRS. But she is most assuredly a fan today for reasons the agency would not understand until it reads this.

CHAPTER 10

With her troubles in the hands of attorneys and Lane's fate in the hands of authorities, at last, Sarah tried to block out the events of her ten-year nightmare. It didn't work, partly because she was such a physical and mental wreck that she couldn't manage a decent night's sleep. Many nights she would awaken in a sweat, swearing that she had heard the phone ring and that it was Lane at the other end. She'd pick up the phone and hear only a buzz. She was as punchdrunk as an old, abandoned prize fighter, and twice as belligerent.

Her hiding place in Olympia was the home of a friend she had met while working with Lane. Susan Brannigan was a woman she could trust, even though she was someone who did not know what Sarah had gone through those ten years. A young businesswoman, Susan was a tower of strength for Sarah in the four months she lived with her—and a tower of strength she needed urgently. Her health was at a low point.

In the devastating years with Lane, she had lost her appetite because of the stress he caused daily from dawn to midnight and beyond. She looked like a skeleton. Since her doctor had told her to stay away from any foods with sugar, she was left with few choices. It didn't matter. She had no appetite anyway. She wasn't anorexic or bulimic, but that was little consolation.

Her enforced imprisonment ended four months later with the blessed news from her attorney that a settlement had been reached with Lane and Darlene and she would be free to resume her life without fear of legal or physical retribution from them. In return for resigning from their bedeviled company and signing away any financial or corporate interest she might have, she would be given ownership of the Seattle home she had paid for with her own funds—and the sweat and blood of ten years of slavery. In addition, the phony adoption she had submitted to in her naivete was null and void, and they no longer had any hold on her.

It was truly "Independence Day" for Sarah. And now she could add another hero to her list of guardian angels. He was Fred Roberson, her attorney, who had carried the torch for her and given her the freedom she had dreamed about but never known. When her case was finally resolved in her favor, he had a confession to make.

"The first time I saw you that December afternoon, my head told me you might be a crackpot and that I should be careful. You must remember that when you came in to see me, you were a walking skeleton, a very sick woman, and you were very depressed. I could see that. But it was obvious you weren't taking drugs or excessive alcohol. I could tell that, too. After we talked awhile and I heard your incredible story, my heart told me you were a good person."

Sarah discovered he was a very strong and devout churchgoer and was incensed over the treatment she had received in life. He became more than her attorney; he became her good friend and a stalwart supporter. If she needed further proof, she received it when he told her from the beginning that he was taking her case without a fee or a retainer.

Although it was "Independence Day" for Sarah, she still felt like a prisoner who has spent most of his life behind bars and is intimidated by sudden freedom. She was now in a new kind of trance.

Lane and his wife had sold their mansion and moved to another city, but she still felt threatened in her home, which had been like a cell for her because it was just across the street from the warden.

The previous summer she had realized the end was near for Lane and his company, so she called a real estate agent to put her house on sale immediately. However, she was cautioned against a quick sale. Her frolicking dog, Suki, had found delight in exercising his incisors and molars on the porch deck and other parts of the house, and they now needed repairs before a sale could be considered. Sarah's bank book was hurting, but she had no choice but to hire a carpenter to do the work. It turned out to be one of the most fortunate decisions she'd made.

That's how she met Ron Holz, a craftsman who was skilled with his hands and who made no pretense about being anything but what he was—a softspoken, kind, generous man about her age who loved doing things for people. He had dancing blue eyes, sandy-colored hair, bushy eyebrows, and an equally bushy mustache. Ron walked with a purpose, and when he stood face to face with someone, chest out, and broad shoulders poised, he was a picture of confidence and self-reliance.

He had just returned from Germany, where he had been born to an American military officer and a German girl. Ron was schooled in both Germany and the United States; 25 of his 34 years had been spent in Germany. He eventually operated his own restaurant in Remagen—until the Bonn government's severe restrictions and immense bureaucracy made it impossible for him to continue.

To Sarah, Ron looked the role of the man she had only dreamed of meeting. He spoke excellent English, mainly because European schools place so much emphasis on English as a second language and because he also attended American schools.

He completed the repair work and said goodbye. Sarah and Ron hadn't talked much on that occasion, because she was away most of the time and the repairs required only one weekend. Despite the work, the house failed to sell that summer and fall, so she took it off the market.

When she gained her independence and went back to Seattle the following spring, she decided to list the house for sale once more. More repairs and a lot of paint were required this time, but now all she had to do was give Ron a call. This time they talked a bit more and, in fact, had a couple of dates that endeared him to Sarah. But it remained a friendship and nothing more at the time.

The second try at selling the house was successful and she moved into a home in Issaquah, just east of Seattle, and settled in to await her long-delayed "new lease on life." She soon discovered it was no cinch. Without a regular paycheck, she had to find work.

Because of her experience in financial management with professionals, she found a position as director of marketing for a Seattle bank, but only two months into her new era of independence, another catastrophe struck.

Sarah became violently ill from food poisoning at a restaurant in a downtown Seattle department store. At a hospital, her doctor and the laboratory indicated the culprit was salmonella. An ordinary person in good health would have been able to overcome the problem in two weeks or so. But her poor health and low resistance made her anything but "an ordinary person." The illness would curse her life for four years and send her to the hospital twice more. She now had a new "warden," and the thought of suicide came frequently. Was she cursed?

Sarah couldn't understand what caused her to reject suicide and go on struggling to find the fervently desired release from pain and fear. In the days of abuse and sexual harassment, she could withdraw from her body at the approach of physical pain. But now the creator of fear was in her own body and mind, and she had no way to escape. If she were too cowardly to die by her own hand, why couldn't nature do the job for her?

Through it all, she had one source of strength, a source that had been planted in her years earlier by Grandma Summers. It was she who introduced Sarah to the power of prayer and faith in God, and now she leaned on the power as never before, whether she realized it or not. If it hadn't been for that, she probably would have made good at last on her impulse to commit suicide.

Give the honors to the Almighty, but credit Ron with a most timely assist. In the midst of her severest illness, he played an even more important role in her life. On a warm summer night in Kirkland, which is across Lake Washington from Seattle, they had dinner outdoors at a shoreside restaurant. It was then that she began telling him some of the details of her decade of slavery and the abuse suffered in childhood, and he told her about his severe financial problems with the dictatorial German bureaucracy over his ill-fated restaurant.

They must have sounded like a distraught couple on one of those let-it-all-hang-out, bleeding-heart talk shows on television. But it was the beginning of a new understanding between them that provided each one with a much needed crutch. A sympathetic listener, at last, for both.

For the longest time, she didn't want to acknowledge that she had fallen in love with Ron. Later, he confessed it had been the same with him. Neither one wanted it to become a romantic entanglement, but neither tried to stop it. Sarah was so afraid of being hurt again that she kept telling herself to back off. He did the same. As a result, they decided to continue to enjoy each other's company whenever they wished, but to put off any permanent commitment. They made love whenever the spirit moved them, but thoughts of marriage were put on hold.

In the meantime, Sarah's relationships with others remained tentative and suspicious. She still would not let anyone but Ron get close to her, because she trusted no one and was mortally afraid to let history repeat itself.

She confided to Ron: "I wish more people would understand that when one has had an abusive relationship over a fairly long period of time, that person is bound to lose the ability or desire to trust others. Or, worse yet, to trust herself. The trust factor has receded into a hidden corner of my soul."

At 25, the year she had gone to work for Lane, she stopped learning how to have a personal relationship and had lost the capacity to love someone without reservation. It was that ability that she would have to learn all over again. Those years of servitude and violence left her very immature, in effect. It had been a decade of damnation. She found that the persons she hurt the most were those who really cared about her—persons who got too close too fast. She didn't want them doing that to her, despite their best intentions. They were entering her space too rapidly. She didn't trust the actions of those who expressed concern or empathy. God forbid if they offered sympathy! Doing so would mean an abrupt end to the "friendship."

Whenever people got too close, she'd "bump them away" somehow, as she put it. It became her suspicious nature to do so. Other women she had known confessed to her that they had a similar problem. Harassed and abused, they *created* opportunities for people to dislike them, as she had done. Why? Because it was the easiest way out, the way to keep them out of your space and from getting too close—a terrible price to pay for good intentions.

Although Sarah enjoyed her position as the bank's marketing director, she knew she had to quit relying on other institutions and go into business on her own. In her executive position with Lane's firm, she had met many health-care professionals, most of them dentists, doctors, and nurses. She knew she could renew relations with most of them, so she decided to go into business as a financial consultant. No Lane-like $70,000 fees this time!

Gradually, she discovered she could help her onetime associates in more ways than financial planning alone. The women particularly understood what she'd been through or had themselves experienced severe abuse or emotional and sexual harassment. Sarah was now in her own element, in the deep caverns of an arena she knew only too well.

Her mistake, however, was to undervalue her services, the direct result of a guilty conscience that grew out of those exorbitant $70,000 fees. In addition, she often refused to take payment in some cases in her zeal to build a new clientele.

Her new credo was: "Show me a consultant who charges only $35 an hour these days or nothing at all, and I'll show you a consultant operating on a starvation budget—as I was."

Some of the health-care professionals she called on saw only the exterior Sarah Summers. To them she was the no-nonsense business professional they wanted to work with or even to emulate. They saw her as a success story. She confessed to Ron:

"What a mirage I was! They seemed to come to me with the attitude that if I taught them what I knew, they, too, would be successful. If only they knew.... Was this Sarah the same Sarah that Lane would describe for all to hear as 'the bitch he rescued from the gutters of life'?"

The "friendship" approach adopted by some of her professional clients was very uncomfortable to Sarah, and she was quick to blame herself for letting it happen. Her distaste for the "let me help you" approach was part of the "victim" mentality that had seized her whole being and her soul. She needed help to heal herself and to have relationships once more that were clean, honest, and had healthy boundaries.

Another factor was that, with the loss of trust in herself and in others, she had forgotten how to cry and how to unleash the hurt and tragedy within herself.

If she had dared cry or show personal emotion in front of Lane, he would make her pay for it. On those occasions when he forced her to have sex, he would never kiss her. He would bite her instead and say: "I would never kiss a whore." It became like a recording tape that ran through her mind with little provocation. She had learned that when abuse destroys your humanity, it's almost impossible to be honestly emotional any more.

Although she had finally escaped the tyranny of a monster, she kept berating herself when her business wasn't doing well or if she failed to win a contract she thought was a cinch. The vicious gremlin in her conscience spoke to her often:

"You're never going to be good enough. You'll never be able to run a successful company."

Although the idea of suicide kept returning, she didn't have the courage nor the strength to take her own life. She became very negative.

On one occasion, Sarah had worked hard to arrange a health-care seminar for professionals and had obtained the services of many reputable speakers. On the morning of the first day of the seminar, she stood once more before the tell-all mirror and spoke aloud:

"Lane was right. I'm a failure. What in hell am I doing? Why would all these people want to come to hear this program? What have I done? I've set everybody up for a flop."

She was crying. Crying! And she didn't realize that the tears were visible evidence that some emotional warmth had been restored to her body. She didn't recognize it then as a small step toward recovery.

The seminar was a huge success. It was well attended and drew the compliments of everyone there. And it was reasonably profitable, although Sarah purposely kept the admission fee very low. Nevertheless, she was a nervous wreck and dissatisfied with herself. She felt guilty about the entire experience. In planning and executing the seminar, she had simply relived everything she no longer wanted to be a part of in helping people make decisions about money. When Ron asked her why she had given up on an organizational talent she had long proved she possessed, she told him:

"I don't want to have anything to do with people's money again. It brings back all the horror and shame of those ten years in captivity. That's why I thought the seminar would fail. I resolved never again to plan another seminar or anything else that resembled what I had done those ten years. I will continue to work as a consultant, but only on a one-on-one basis under conditions I can control."

In the meantime, Ron and Sarah made a decision. Marriage was not yet in the cards, but they decided they would toss all their blessings and woes into one basket and live together.

The idea was: Let's give it a try and see if we're meant for each other. What can we lose? It was like two cases from 201 Abnormal Psychology. Despite her continuing poor health, her consulting business took a turn for the better and Ron was doing well after going into business for himself building incredible, artistic furniture and cabinetry and selling a new line of air purifiers.

Sarah didn't hesitate to credit Ron with a most important turning point in her life and in their relationship. Because of the bitterness that sex had brought her, she had decided she would never again permit any man to invade her innermost world again. She was still having nightmares over the traumatic invasions forced upon her by Lane, and she would sometimes awaken screaming at the thought that he was once again forcing her legs apart and bludgeoning her with his terrible weapon. At times the monster in her nightmares was her father. They were interchangeable.

By the time they had decided to live together, Ron knew the intimate details of Sarah's childhood and her years of debasement at Lane's hands. He made no demands and bided his time. Sarah was almost uncontrollably nervous and apprehensive the first time she realized she and Ron were headed for sexual intercourse. In her ill-fated marriage and again with Lane, she had steeled herself each time the specter of sex approached. On all those occasions, she had fled her body to avoid the sensations of pain and violence, so she had never experienced what books, magazines, and movies had depicted as the delirious joy of sex.

Ron was gentle. He was patient and understanding, and it was immediately obvious that he knew the importance of love, foreplay, and tenderness in the sex act. The first time was only partly satisfying to Sarah, but for the first time in her life, she found that the "joy of sex" was more than a come-on for soft-cover pornography. In time, Ron helped her overcome her abhorrence of sex, although the nightmares persisted for many months.

Once, early on, in the midst of an amorous embrace in bed, she suddenly began screaming: "No! No! No! Lane, you son of a bitch! Leave me alone!" Ron shook her, realizing that the passion of the moment had caused her to lapse into a living nightmare. He understood, and they put off their lovemaking for a time.

A few months after they moved in together, another episode in her erratic life occurred to signal she was at last on the road to real recovery. "The road" is an appropriate way to put it.

She was returning home after a most successful consultation one day and driving on the Hobart-Issaquah Road, which took her to her home in the countryside. Suddenly, as if she had been struck by a bolt of lightning, she felt a rush of emotion—the feeling that she was returning to her body. For the first time in years, she felt that she had come alive, that this was finally the real Sarah in her own body. She knew she was not the first to experience it, because she had heard and read about others going through it. It wasn't easy to explain to Ron, but she tried:

"Because of the pain and abuse I had had to endure so much of my earlier life, I had deserted my body and had gone through the eerie feeling of watching myself move, talk, and act. Until that moment on the Hobart-Issaquah Road, I had felt that everything in me had been shut off, except the strange ability to witness my actions from outside my body. Before the incident on the road, I had not felt physically present at work or anywhere else. It was not really a trance. My heart wasn't palpitating and I didn't have an adrenalin rush. My body simply had no sensation. All that changed from the moment I remember so vividly while driving on the Issaquah-Hobart Road. And, most important of all, from that day forward I have been in my body physically and have been aware of all that was going on around me.

"To this day I have not lost my fear of pain and violence and would move quickly into my shell if hurt or attacked in some way. But in the main I am 'fully there' and experiencing so many things I once blocked out. For example, I once went along with conversations or frustrations in a group, nodding compliance and refusing to speak my mind. But after the road incident, I lost my shyness and I am no longer afraid to speak up when I disagree with someone or feel the urge to make a point, no matter how controversial. It's now a privilege to get angry when the spirit moves me. Others will take me as I am or not all."

Ron asked no more questions. The deep smile on his face told her he understood and was as happy as she was over the miracle on the Issaquah-Hobart Road.

In recent years, Sarah has often startled groups at meetings or seminars with statements they didn't expect to hear. They may not agree with her, but now, at least, they know she is speaking her mind and not agreeing with them for the sake of being liked. She no longer has to please everyone because it's "the right thing to do." That philosophy caused her so much misery and has caused women so much distress through the ages that it deserves permanent burial.

Her Mom had to subjugate herself in every way to "please" her philandering husband, no matter how foul his behavior. And Sarah had had to do the same for her Dad, her first husband, and, finally, Lane.

In their foolish obedience to the Muse of Pleasing Man, women the world over have not only wound up displeasing themselves but displeasing men, as well. It took Sarah half a lifetime to find a man like Ron, who treated her as an equal and who knew the real meaning of love and patience and kindness. And because he offers those human gifts to her every day of their lives, she cannot wait to offer him gifts in kind.

CHAPTER 11

One more test of strength remained for Sarah before she could say with confidence that she would never permit anyone, male or female, to intimidate her and expose her to more abuse, whether emotional, physical, or sexual. The test came from a surprising source.

Sarah knew she would never be totally free to enjoy success in her business and personal life until she could conquer her physical and mental problems, or at least minimize them so they would not interfere. It was long past time to turn herself in to competent professionals to get treatment for her ailing body and mind. However, in her anxiety to find psychiatric counseling and mental and physical therapy, she ran into another "situation."

May was a chiropractor she had met at one of her meetings with health-care professionals. They compared notes, and in the beginning Sarah found her to be understanding and personable. They made an agreement. Sarah would provide her with the management advice she needed in her chiropractic practice and May would give Sarah the treatments she needed for an aching back and the nerve and muscular problems that had dogged her for so long. Sarah also needed frequent massages to relieve the stress that was still with her. No money would change hands; it was to be an even exchange.

May was decidedly on the heavy side, more than 200 pounds, and very strong. Once a week for four months she worked over Sarah's body in a very effective and professional manner, and Sarah began to feel herself approaching normalcy again and distancing herself from stress. Nothing untoward happened at those sessions until the fourth month.

Gloria, a friend whose judgment Sarah admired and who had also been treated by May, met her for lunch one day and asked how the workouts were going.

"Oh, wonderful! I feel so much better after those sessions, and I can just feel the worries peeling away."

"You know, of course, that she has her eye on you, don't you?"

"What are you talking about? Our association is purely professional. I help her manage her business and, in return, she gives me the physical treatment I need very much. What's wrong with that?"

"Oh, come on, Sarah. You know what I mean. You know that May is, well, not like, you know, other women."

All the "you knows" were giving Sarah a pain in the seat.

"Why are you stumbling around for words. Of course I know. May told me herself in one of our business sessions. She's a lesbian. Her family knows it. Her friends know it. But why should that matter? She's terrific at what she does. And that's all I want or expect of her."

"Sure, but did you know she, well, that she sort of, you know, cares for you as more than a friend?"

Sarah couldn't think of what to say, so she said nothing, but she had already indicated to Gloria that she had had no idea that May had other intentions.

"You mean you didn't know she, you know, felt that way about you?"

"Of course I didn't know. And I don't care. The whole thing is absolutely ridiculous. I don't want to get involved with a lesbian or anyone else, for that matter!"

Sarah didn't realize she was almost shouting in protest to the whole idea. Now, who in hell needed an extra worry like that one? Was Gloria just another busybody who liked to invent trouble, even for a friend? Or was there something more to all of this than Sarah was willing to admit? May had made no advances. If she had, Sarah would have ended their association on the spot. She resolved to give May the benefit of a doubt and to believe that Gloria had been wrong in her assumption.

May had been to Sarah's home on business many times in those four months, and not once did she indicate she had any intentions other than to serve as a health counselor and chiropractor. However, Sarah had to admit that on the last two or three visits, she was beginning to get the impression that it was she who was the health and physical counselor. May would stay for hours, long past the usual time she spent on earlier visits.

Sarah didn't mind the lengthening stays. It was the litany of lamentations from May that became her major concern.

She began telling Sarah about her problems at home and going into long, interminable crying spells. Sarah thought she had problems! After acknowledging she was a lesbian, May went into her difficulties with her mother and stepfather in a monotonous crying jag that taxed Sarah's patience. Why was she telling her all this? She was the health expert, not Sarah. Exasperated, Sarah told her it didn't matter to her that she was a lesbian, although she made it clear that it wasn't her sexual preference.

May made a habit of phoning her frequently in the daytime and in the evening. On several occasions, she would call late at night to ask if Sarah would join her for a party. Sarah was irritated but tried not to reflect it in turning her down.

Once she had devoted an entire weekend to a new client and, after 20 hours of hard work, she told Ron that if anyone called for her, he should say she had gone to bed for the evening. It was 8 pm on a Sunday evening, and she was exhausted. At 11:30, the phone rang and Ron picked it up. It was May. She and a friend took turns talking to him. Both laughed and giggled throughout and were obviously soused. They wanted to know where they could go for a drink and wanted Sarah to join them. Ron directed them to a restaurant nearby and made excuses for Sarah.

On another evening, Sarah was reading on the living-room sofa, with her dog, Sam (as in Samantha), nuzzling against her contentedly. She and Ron had acquired Sam to replace Suki, who had gone to her reward the year before. Suddenly, Sam leaped from the sofa and began barking at the window. Sarah looked out and saw faint shadows moving away and quickly out of sight. Sam continued barking and growling for at least five minutes more, and Sarah had to put some food in her bowl to coax the dog to stop.

Sarah's heart was pounding with fear and she knew she was on the verge of another out-of-body experience. Sam had never acted that way unless she heard, smelled, or saw someone outside the house. Ron came home a short time later and calmed her down. He searched the premises and found some suspicious footprints in the flower garden, but not much else.

When she mentioned the incident to Gloria the next day, an awkward silence ensued.

After searching Sarah's face for an indication of irritation or anger, Gloria tested the waters.

"Sarah, I think you're still put out with me for what I said about May. Do you really want me to tell you what I'm thinking?"

"Holy Toledo, Gloria. Of course I want you to say what you're thinking. So what are you thinking? And don't pull any punches."

"Well, have you considered the possibility that it was May and one or two of her friends who were snockered and just playing Peeping Tom on you? I may as well tell you what's on my mind and what others have noticed, too, even if you don't—or don't want to. I think May is jealous of Ron and sees him as a sort of competitor. So there. I've said it, and I'm glad."

"Oh, Gloria, you're dreaming! She wouldn't do anything as stupid as that, now, would she?" Sarah searched Gloria's face for an answer, then repeated, slowly: "Would she?"

A moment later, Sarah regained her composure, calling the whole story preposterous. But after she left Gloria, she couldn't erase from her mind the suspicion her friend had planted there.

At their next scheduled session, Sarah and May behaved as if nothing unusual had happened between them—and perhaps nothing had. Now, however, the monster of suspicion attended the session and invaded Sarah's mind. Two, three, and four sessions went by, and she grew more uncomfortable with May each time. The hands-on treatments had never bothered her before, but now she had to control her body and her thoughts whenever May laid a strong hand on her. The ministrations were no longer soothing; her nerves and muscles now recoiled at the touch. Sarah wondered what May might do in retaliation if she accused her of the thoughts Gloria had put into her mind.

She was afraid she might explode and even become violent if she told May abruptly to knock it off. Besides, the chiropractor had been so successful as a healer that she had helped Sarah immensely, physically and mentally. Of course, Sarah had helped her, too. With her advice and planning, May's practice jumped from six patients a week to 40 or more. Besides, Sarah had no proof of Gloria's intimations.

Had it not been for the mutual benefits involved, Sarah might have declared "Enough!" a lot sooner.

In what turned out to be their last business session, May startled her.

"Sarah, do you think I'm in love with you?"

For a moment, Sarah was speechless. It was designed as a question, and a strangely worded one at that, but it came out more as a statement of fact. Apparently May had been talking with Gloria and other mutual friends again and was aware that Sarah knew she was interested in more than a business association in their relationship.

"What are you talking about? What's going on?" That's all Sarah could manage to say at the moment.

"Oh, nothing. I was just wondering."

Sarah realized she had to say something more definitive than "What's going on?" So she seized the bull by the horns, to use an appropriate description. Now that May had put her own words to Gloria's suspicions, Sarah had to act firmly. With visions of the abusive slavery she had succumbed to at the hands of a cruel father and a brutal employer, she gritted her teeth and let it all pour out.

"May, you're not my type. I'm not interested in you that way, nor in any woman." She was trying not to be rude, but she couldn't help it. May fell silent, offering no rebuttal. That was the end of the conversation, and Sarah left without another word. When she reached her car, she was relieved that she didn't try to force a showdown, mainly because she had heard what slighted homosexuals might do when repudiated.

Three weeks later Sarah had to visit May's office to deliver a brochure she had been working on for her, and she hoped May wouldn't be there. No such luck.

"I need to speak with you, Sarah, and I'm not willing to do that in a telephone conversation. I'd like to know when you can fit me into your busy schedule so you and I can have a conversation."

"Well, it's possible." Sarah was hedging, but she suddenly felt helpless before this giant of a woman. Once again she had fleeting and disturbing visions of being locked into another abusive and violent situation like those that had cursed her past.

"What does that mean?"

"It means I have a lot going on in my life right now, May, and I'm not willing to have a conversation that may be upsetting."

"But I thought we were friends?"

"Yes, I thought we were friends, too, and friends support each other. Right now, I don't want to have that type of conversation." How in hell was Sarah going to get out of this sticky situation that somehow had taken on a threatening tone? She began to feel as she always had before Lane struck her or pinned her to a wall with his hands around her neck. Or her father approached with a terrible sneer, razor strop poised above his head. Sarah's body was sweating, and she was afraid it showed.

Fortunately, May backed down, choosing not to press the issue at that time.

"Well, maybe we can talk Tuesday when we have our regular meeting."

The business of the brochure needed to be settled, but Sarah suddenly had no further interest in the brochure or in the "friendship."

"Maybe Tuesday. Gotta go. See you later."

As she was walking away, May said: "You haven't been in my office in three weeks."

Now emboldened, Sarah answered flippantly: "Yup, and I'm feeling great, thank you."

That was the end of the convenient exchange of services and the business relationship. There was no way in hell Sarah was going to return for sessions with her. She never saw her again. In place of the friendship she had once felt for her was a fear that this massive, ultra-strong woman would not leave her alone.

Although she wanted no part of an intimate relationship with May, Sarah knew instinctively that her concern had little or nothing to do with May's lesbianism. She had known many women and men who made no attempt to hide their homosexuality and she had been on friendly terms with them, fearing nothing. But with May, she saw the beginnings of the same "disease" that had made her life miserable—the threat of physical violence and abuse that would leave her defenseless if she didn't sever relations in time. In May's case, at least, Sarah was able to do so without absorbing a vicious beating or emotional whipping.

When she returned home that night, Sarah fairly collapsed into her favorite overstuffed chair, dropped her brief case to the floor, took big Sam into her lap, and began a smile that gradually turned into laughter that was so hearty she put her hand to her mouth, almost embarrassed. What a load off her mind! What a great sense of relief possessed her. And how blessed it was for her to feel that way.

She needed no explanation for her newest delivery from oppression. Now, she felt, she was finally ready to get on with her life, to explore at last what it meant to be happy, to be loved, to love back, and to do it all without chains.

CHAPTER 12

As her health improved and the stress in her life diminished, thanks to Ron's gentle ministrations and the end of the May episode and the last threat to her freedom, a more relaxed Sarah measured her past and the plight of the Summers clan with a more forgiving eye. She surveyed the damage to a family shattered by violence, abuse, drugs, and alcohol like an infantry colonel grieving over the dead and wounded in a battle he could not avoid. But now she found a small measure of solace in realizing that the disasters in her family were invited by forces they could not control. It solved nothing, but it eased her conscience.

What different lives could the six Summerses have led if their actions or failure to act had not been influenced by severe physical, emotional, and sexual abuse, by chronic alcoholism, by the easy presence of booze, and by the quick access and free use of drugs? Had she judged her parents, her brother, and her two sisters too harshly, or did they deserve the antagonism she had felt most of her life? Finally, was her family a reflection of the situation in most other families in modern society, or was hers an exception to the rule?

She began adopting a clinical view of each of the members in the Summers clan, perhaps to understand her own distressed life by analyzing theirs. In groups of women who now recognized her courage and willingness to lay her life out on the table, Sarah found herself saying things like this, without embarrassment:

"Take my Dad, for example. In his heart of hearts, he may have been a good, caring human being at one time, but when you grow up in a harsh environment, such as we did—and I know his was even harsher than ours—whom do you trust? He had a father that was abusive and unkind to him. In fact, his father tried his damnedest to prevent his birth with an assault on his wife, so deranged was he. How can you expect a child to develop normally with that kind of a start in life?"

When Sarah was born, Dad—Ken Summers—was a very happy and attentive father. Mom told her that when she was a toddler and up to the time she was a bit more than 2, he was wonderful with her. Sarah was his pride and joy, his beloved little girl the first two years of her life. Then her brother Steve was born, and Dad changed almost overnight. Steve's arrival couldn't have been the reason, but the heavy drinking began simultaneously and the womanizing started in earnest. Had his terribly abusive childhood finally caught up with him? Whatever it was, he became a violent, drunken tyrant, abusive not only to his children in subsequent years but to his wife, as well.

In the few times Sarah saw and talked to her father since fleeing Lethbridge, she always felt she was once again the 7-or 8-year-old child he flogged whenever she displeased him.

She could not have an adult conversation with him because she never had that relationship with him. In the few visits she had with him in later years, she was forced mentally and emotionally to go back to being that small child and realized she had never healed from all the wounds. Nor had he. Who or what was to blame? He never apologized for his abusive behavior nor did Sarah ask him to. Would it have made a difference if he had? Sarah doubted it would.

Although she knew he hadn't changed and showed no sign of doing so, she suspected he never would. But she remained ready to give him the benefit of a doubt and say that his violent behavior was prompted to some degree by the violent behavior he suffered at the hands of his father.

Most of all, Sarah wanted to be much closer to her mother, Lettie Summers, and become a friend, rather than the errant daughter she was usually considered to be. But it would not be an easy transformation.

In her own way, Mom had been a sort of guardian angel for Sarah. With her mother in mind, she told herself that people tend to be most critical and demanding of those who play the role of teacher, like Mom, and actually extend the personal boundaries of those in their care. From what Sarah had been able to learn from relatives and friends who knew her well in her early years, she knew that Mom was an admirable child. She was constantly involved in helping others and she was remarkably athletic and good at whatever sport she tried. Whether it was hockey, figure skating, or even hunting down and capturing rattlesnakes, for goodness' sake, she was always the first one to try something new. And doing very well at it.

To this day, whenever Sarah watches figure-skating championships, she sees Mom in her mind's eye in the role of a top contender and eventually the winner of the Gold Medal! It also causes Sarah to wonder what her life could have been—and Sarah's, as well—if she had followed her dream. And Sarah knew for sure that the life of a figure-skater was her dream.

She had no doubt that Mom was happy with her children for the most part, although the rocky journey to the present hadn't exactly been a happy one nor one she might have desired. But, for all the heartaches, disappointments, and violence she and Sarah endured, Mom was a champion in her daughter's eyes. Sarah could say that despite the fact that they had not had what most persons would describe as a successful mother-daughter relationship.

As she looked back over her life, Sarah was saddened by the choices her mother made because they did not fulfill the promise of the person she truly was. Her health was a reflection of those choices. She had many ailments that needed constant medication and which masked the secret desires she held close to her heart. Her ailments were typical of the disorders plaguing those who manage to survive violence, abuse, and a variety of serious addictions. They are the trademarks of physical, mental, and emotional injustices that scar the soul forever, as they did Mom's and Sarah's.

In the case of the Summers clan, were all those ailments the product of the violence, abuse, alcohol, and drug addictions?

Sarah could answer, as she did with her therapist and her closest friends: "Without a doubt! But we are not alone. Many, many people have these disorders and the accompanying hidden or repressed memories and are willing to seek help for them. From what I have observed, a great many people with chronic fatigue syndrome have been through abusive, physical, emotional, and sexual abuse."

In her mother's case, Sarah could not help sobbing as she said: "For a long time, I didn't like Mom. I put up with her and I was angry with her most of the time, because she wasn't there for me so often when I needed her most. Of course, the reason was that she was busy working. She had no choice. She had to work. But at other times she wasn't there for me when she *was* present. By that, I mean she didn't protect us from my father's constant abuse and beatings. She was involved in doing things that are unimportant. When you lose sight of what is most important in life, you become a different person. Mom seems at last to recognize what is truly important and reordering her life accordingly."

Of all members of her family, Sarah was most sympathetic with her brother Steve, who is in a "soul-searching period of his life."

No one in the family and, in fact, no person she had ever known, had absorbed as much abuse in a short lifetime as he had—from her father first and foremost and then from others in the drug world. But he has been sober and free of drugs for more than a decade and is determined to stay that way and remake his life. He would like to marry and have children, but he knows he cannot and must not have children.

Sarah acknowledged that needed explaining. It isn't because of physical reasons that he can't have children. It's because the ugly scars in his memory from all those beatings and from the legacy of violence he inherited remind him of what he's capable of doing to children if he had them. And having gone through much of the same thing, Sarah understands why he is not the type of person who can or should have children. It's the reason Sarah also is reluctant to bear children. She and Steve and many people like them are afraid history will repeat itself with them.

Sarah calls Steve a living miracle, who should not be alive today. In his drug-infested existence, he fell off a train traveling more than 50 miles an hour and survived. She knows of at least two dozen instances in which he was severely hurt in deadly scrapes or accidents. It must be that he was destined to survive to contribute something of value to society.

Despite his violent past, he has retained his sense of humor, his consideration for others, and his gift for writing poetry. Steve is in the process of forming a greeting-card company to take advantage of his poetic skill. Imagine what cards can be turned out by a person who's been through what he has.

Physically, Steve has many impairments, no surprise for someone who has lived a life of abuse and who seems to have more lives than a whole family of cats. In addition to spinal arthritis, he suffers from a tightening of all the joints—knees, wrists, fingers, toes, and elbows. What an inheritance he drew from his father.

Is there a possibility Steve and Sarah and all other victims of family violence and abuse could be cured of their mental ailment and erase their past?

Sarah's emphatic answer was that such a person never outlives it. She was reminded of those unfortunates who lived through the horrors of the wartime concentration camps. They never get over it. They may go on to live productive lives, but there's a part of them that has been genetically changed by the violent experience. That's the reason she, Steve, and others who have been through abusive years cannot go back to what might be called a normal life, whatever that is. Their minds, genes, and bodies have been altered for all time.

Were Steve's frequent brushes with death willful? Was he, like Sarah, suicidal?

Totally, in her estimation. Steve treaded that fine line that separates brilliance and insanity. Some days he's brilliant in what he says, what he writes, what he does. On other days he seems to be on the line or over it. One could never know which day will produce what condition. And Sarah didn't think he does either.

The family member Sarah understands least is her sister Elaine, mainly because she has seen her only a few times since the hasty departure from Canada. In their early years in Lethbridge, they got along very well and played together often. Sarah cannot account for the hatred that developed, but she is certain the severe abuse dealt Elaine by her father had most to do with her deep antagonism toward Sarah. Another contributing reason was that Elaine blamed Sarah for Mom's sudden flight from the family home in Canada, with Sarah and Marian in tow.

Elaine was a whining child, who cried instantly whenever she couldn't have her way. On one of the few occasions Sarah saw Elaine in recent years, there was an even greater deterioration of the relationship between them. Against her better judgment, Sarah had made a Christmas trip by plane to see her father, brother, and sister in Canada. Elaine picked her up at the Calgary airport and began the two-hour drive to the new family home. En route, Elaine said to Sarah without taking her eye off the road:

"I'm allowing you to come up to see Dad only if you promise you will not hurt him again."

Sarah was in no mood to start an oral battle, so she said nothing. But the words were forming in her mind: "If I don't hurt *him!*" What an interesting concept! Was Elaine so intimidated by the incessant abuse at the hands of their father that she had lost all memory? That had to be it. The two young women avoided conversation the day Sarah spent there, and that suited Sarah fine. Once again the brief time she spent with her father on that visit was awkward and very uncomfortable. He continued to treat her as he had when she was a child. Only her reacquaintance with her grandfather was pleasant and made the uneasy trip worth it.

Once later on in Seattle, Steve invited both sisters to his home for a party to celebrate the fifth anniversary of his joining Alcoholics Anonymous and controlling his alcoholism. He had more than a party in mind, because he had not told Elaine that Sarah had been invited, too. On entering the house, Elaine was startled to see Sarah there, but she moved toward her and gave her a hug. A few minutes later she cornered Steve and became hysterical, blaming him for tricking her into the meeting and screaming: "I will not see her! I will not talk to her! I will not have anything to do with her!" She and her boyfriend left immediately thereafter as she unleashed a torrent of four-letter words at Steve and Sarah.

Elaine cut herself off from all members of the family, except her father. That was especially strange to Sarah, when one considered the abuse Elaine had suffered at his hand. She wanted nothing to do with Mom, Steve, or Marian because, she let it be known, they chose to have a relationship with Sarah, such as it was in each case.

Sarah still had no idea why Elaine continued the hate campaign against her. Steve and Mom didn't understand it. Sarah wrote her letters and tried calling her on the phone, but Elaine would not answer the letters or the calls.

The only member of the family whose severe problems could not be laid to violence and abuse was Marian, but she was a victim, nevertheless, of factors that grew out of violence and abuse.

Sarah realized that Marian was a child whose birth was a miracle. Mom was told by doctors that under no conditions should she ever have another child. She was extremely thin and dangerously under weight. She had kidney stones and a kidney infection. She had other problems Sarah couldn't put names to. Her father knew all that, but Mom got pregnant anyway, and Marian was born, but barely.

Little Marian had "soft bones" and virtually all the ailments a child can have. Her childhood was a succession of illnesses. It should have surprised no one that she grew up completely spoiled by Mom and by Dad, who called her his favorite, his Boo Boo Bear. That's the reason she escaped his abuse—that and her continuing illnesses and the fact that he didn't have much of a chance to abuse her, because she was only 5 when she left Lethbridge with Mom and Sarah.

She grew up as the baby, and she's still the baby. Marian still demands all the attention she can get and doesn't care to help others. She continues to behave as an alcoholic might, even though she doesn't drink. Her two children often feel the sting of her temper, no surprise in the Summers family. Marian has a myopic view of life. Sarah doesn't understand her and probably never will. And yet, for strange reasons she cannot fathom, she can still sympathize with Marian's myopic view of life.

Is Marian, who somehow escaped the childhood abuse her brother and sisters suffered continually, an exception in Sarah's view of the American family?

Sarah responded with a definite "No." In one way or another, a child born into a highly abusive family reaps the shrapnel from that explosive family, as Marian did. Call the rest of the family "carriers." Evidence of the "Summers disease" can be found in countless American and Canadian families, maybe a majority of them. Sarah pondered the cases of many of her friends who have an abusive relationship with their husbands and they have children no different than her sister Marian. They're no different than the way her brother Steve and sister Elaine behaved—and the way she behaved—in the childhood and teen-age years.

In Sarah's mind, the Great American Tragedy will not be found in novels. It resides in families, and the mounting abuse, violence, alcoholism, and drug addiction will make it worse—unless people everywhere rise and demand that we put an end to it before it puts an end to us.

But is there no hope for the "diseased"? Sarah had tried to find an answer to the question for a very long time, but the answer was always the same. Perhaps. Just perhaps. If her brother and sisters knew and felt the pain of what Sarah had been through, their relationship might have been far different than it was and Sarah might begin to understand them and what they have suffered, as well. Have all the Summerses learned the healing power of forgiveness? Not yet, Sarah knew. But, who knows? There may still be time....

EPILOGUE

As she began her 40th year, the future looked as promising for Sarah Summers as the past had been degrading. Maybe it was true that life begins at 40. At least she could hope so. Was she cured physically and mentally? She wasn't sure, but at least she had a strong desire to help cure others who may have fallen into the same trap that imprisoned her. Her hope was that, by helping to cure them, she might make her own cure permanent. What is it that's said about doctors? "Physician, heal thyself...."

Sarah had retained her penchant for critical self-analysis, mainly because of her innate fear that the violence and chaos of her earlier life might return. She acknowledged that the largest share of credit for her brighter outlook belonged to Ron, whose kindness, gentleness, and understanding in all things had caused her to revise her anger toward the male animal. Sarah called him the most skilled therapist she had known, although he professed to know nothing about therapy. Maybe that's the reason he merited the label.

If only she had met him years sooner, he could have spared her so much agony and so many tears.

Sex was an evil, dirty word before Ron came along with his infinite patience to show her that it can be the most beautiful and blissful act a woman can enjoy. For the longest time, she rebelled against that enjoyment. The memory of her father's abuse and

Lane's brutal treatment lingered but was now buffered in her daily existence. She didn't mind saying that honest and caring love eventually succeeded in chasing much of the hate implanted in her through three decades of abuse and harassment. She knew Ron's ministrations had succeeded the first time it was she, and not he, who initiated the act of love. That glorious happening was a fantastic revelation to her, as it must have been to him.

Sarah owed much to a few others, as well. If it had not been for the faith Grandma Summers instilled in her in her earliest years and her insistence on teaching Sarah the power of prayer, she wouldn't have made it through the decade of slavery under Lane nor those frequent times of despair in which she seriously contemplated suicide. At 40, she was still devoted to prayer and was sure that Grandma knew many of her messages to heaven were addressed to her. Sarah didn't care if that sounded terribly melodramatic. It was the truth. Sarah never apologized for acknowledging the gifts from Grandma and from God.

Her relationships with other people were improving dramatically, primarily because her attitude had changed dramatically. Until recently, she admitted, she was not honest with her feelings and if she became upset over something disturbing, she let it simmer inside her and said nothing to anyone—not even admitting to herself that she had been treated shabbily.

She knew the healing process would probably be a lifelong event, but her new freedom from hurt brought a curious but welcome new development in her. It loosened her tongue, dismissed her shyness, and removed the shackles from her brain. It was as if she were meeting herself for the first time. She was certain that those who had known her earlier and met her again after an interval of a few years must have felt the same way.

One example came when she met with a group of five business women to consider formation of a dental-consulting group. She was familiar with two of them but was not acquainted with the three others. When they decided to tell each other something about themselves and what their "passion in life was," they asked Sarah to speak first.

She told them some of the details of her consulting work, then let the words flow as if she had suddenly been released from captivity.

"I earn my livelihood as a financial consultant to health-care professionals—dentists, doctors, nurses, and others. That's what I do because that's what I was trained to do. But it's not my passion. I thought long and hard about this meeting tonight and whether I wanted to attend. The reason I hesitated is that I didn't know if I wanted to show you the person I really am or the person I wanted you to know. I made the decision that I want to be vulnerable to you and to tell you what my true passion in life is."

She told them about her years of virtual slavery, of abuse, and of violence in a dysfunctional family and finally at the hands of a brute. She told them about the shattered remains of what was once a family of six Summerses. Was it really Sarah talking that way? She didn't know what was urging her on, but she couldn't stop. She told them she was working on a book that would reveal her life story with all the wrinkles and warts and bleeding, the purpose being to help other women in similar plight and also to open the eyes of men who were mistreating the women in their lives. Quoting herself, she said:

"When you come from a background where money is a luxury and only wealthy people are truly happy, you can't expect much. Until I graduated from high school, I never had anything brand new. We shopped at the Goodwill store. We didn't own a car. We didn't even own a washer and dryer. Each Saturday I was responsible for lugging 20 pounds of laundry to the laundromat. Because my mother had to work, thanks to a philandering father who drank up whatever he might earn, I was the oldest and the real mother to two sisters and a brother. I didn't want the responsibility, but I had no choice. And because I was the surrogate mother, my father blamed me for whatever went wrong and even if nothing went wrong. I was beaten mercilessly and often by a drunken father who loved only himself.

"As a tot, I loved my father. But by the time I was 4 or 5, the love had changed to fear and hate. His violent actions, like the time he purposely slammed a car door on my hand and broke it, and the many beatings and constant abuse he subjected me to destroyed my trust in him. That's the most important point. I lost trust in him, and when a child has that happen, her small world collapses.

"Some of the blame must go to my mother. She did not abuse us nor beat us, but we had little trust in her, as well, because she was seldom available to us and she did not come to our aid when we most needed her. At least she had an acceptable excuse. She had to work, because my father did not provide for his family. And she herself was a terrible victim of his incessant beatings.

"Is it any wonder that when I met a businessman who offered me what appeared to be my first responsible job, I took it eagerly—and in ten years of slavery paid a terrible price because we women had been taught that our main goal in life is to please men, no matter what the cost?

"Right here in our own state of Washington, we have had a United States senator and a Governor who have made national headlines for their sexual harassment of women. It's true that both men saw their political careers ruined, but what other penalties did they have to pay? Both have retired or will retire on very comfortable pensions. They've lost nothing else. But what happened to the women they harassed and who had to endure severe public embarrassment? They not only lost their jobs. They lost something far more important, something they may take years to overcome, if ever. The Governor and Senator are

only two of the notorious tormentors, abusers, and harassers.
Even a President and countless members of Congress have been
perpetrators. It is truly a national disease.

"Abuse takes three forms in our society—physical, sexual, and
emotional. The first two are cruel enough, but it's emotional abuse
that is the worst of all and lingers for years and years. The young
women abused by the Senator and the Governor said afterward
that the emotional scars were the most serious damages by far.
They were so humiliated that they were afraid to tell anyone about
their horrible experience for a long time. That was my experience,
too. I told no one about the continued abuse I suffered, mainly
because I was ashamed and thought I wouldn't be believed. Or,
worse, that I might even be blamed for what happened in this
man's world.

"Young women particularly don't want to report sex abusers
when they see what often happens to those who are caught. Just
recently, a professor at a Western university was accused of sexual
assault by two co-eds, and the expectation is that several other
women students may file similar charges. What action did the university take against the professor? He was offered early retirement—*early retirement, for God's sake, and no other punishment!*

"The pernicious nature of emotional abuse is that no one can see
it, except the victim. We live in a culture that can't see it or refuses
to see it, and therefore emotional abuse has no substance, no visible
evil face. Just recently we had the case of the little girl whose
deranged mother was convicted of murder. The foster parents
knew it might happen, because they could see the child's behavior
change for the worse when authorities ordered her returned to her
biological mother. The government workers didn't recognize the
emotional abuse in the child, because, as I said, it is not recognized
by our society.

"That was the situation with me in those awful years with Lane. People couldn't see what was happening to me. I hid it and protected myself, because I would not let the world know what was going on. Like the women harassed by the Senator and the Governor, I was too embarrassed to tell and I feared the humiliation of it all. In my case, I also feared the harm that would come to me if I told. It could have cost me my life. Worse than the physical or sexual abuse to me was the threat of the emotional abuse—the unending tirades, the vicious insults, the shouted epithets, the reminders that I was nothing more than a 'stupid whore.' That kind of abuse is totally demoralizing.

"Because men still dominate the world, it will take more to set things right than simply organizing women to demand better treatment. We have to get the message to the men. Maybe we finally have a way to do it. You've all heard about the national men's movement called Promise Keepers. It has attracted more than a million men to stadiums around the country to hear speakers tell them they should be better fathers and family providers. But it's an all-male event, wherever it takes place. I wish they would invite me to tell all of them a story they need to hear if the men and women of the future are to live as real equals.

"So there you have the gist of the story I want to tell in my book. Maybe it will help create a healing process and save others from the hell that robbed me of the first 39 years of my life."

Sarah said she had been speaking to the five women with her eyes to the floor much of the time. When she looked up, all five were crying. She was alarmed.

"What's going on?"

"Oh," said one woman, dabbing her eyes with a handkerchief, "you're so real!"

"Thank you. I guess the way I look at it is that the Velveteen Rabbit is my favorite story. The only time you're real is when your fur is all rubbed off. My fur has been rubbed off now for a very long time. I feel that I have been totally exposed. Everything that I might have believed in as a child has been shattered. I've had to restructure my life like a sculptor starting anew with an untouched batch of clay. In my naivete, I've permitted some people to take advantage of me, and I'm just not going to let that happen any more, no matter what it takes.

"I want to tell whoever will listen that if you have not walked in other people's shoes, you cannot make a judgment about them. And I want to tell everyone that my experience has shown me that each person should relate to others only with love and tenderness, never with violence or words that tell them how wicked or horrible they are. My reason for being here and telling my story is really simple. By telling you what happened to me, I hope I can prevent it from happening to you and others and your children. That's my passion. That's what I want to do."

Sarah was surprised by her own words, but she felt a sudden escape from all the demons that had pursued her most of her life. It was like being reborn on the spot, and all five women bolstered her morale with their kind words and their tears.

The meeting was a turning point for Sarah. She realized the only way to deal honestly with others was to let it all hang out and to dispense with the phony rhetoric and pretenses. As a result, she has made many new friends in recent months—and revived friendships with others, like John and Barbara, whom she had met years earlier when they wanted help on a retirement plan. John had been a Marine Corps pilot in the Vietnam war and had flown several missions in helicopters, taking men in and out of battle zones. He survived the war and later became a lieutenant colonel in charge of procuring copters, tanks, and other equipment for the Pentagon.

John had retired from the service and returned to Seattle. When he and Barbara called Sarah for more help with retirement details, she went to their home. Both said they were pleasantly surprised to meet "the new Sarah Summers." Like so many others, they, too, had been turned off by Lane's outrageous fees and said they would have withdrawn much sooner had it not been for Sarah's help. They insisted on knowing what had changed her so much over the years. As she had with her five women friends a few weeks earlier, she told them what had happened to her, pulling no punches. Like the women, John and Barbara were crying when she had finished. And so was Sarah. Again, the tears were a moral, emotional victory—the tears that were withheld for years by fear!

"I remember the very first time I met you," John said. "I thought, 'My God, what an attractive woman.' But what was so weird was that there was nothing sexual about you. It was such a turnoff. A lot of other people felt the same way about you, and now I understand. You did turn that part of yourself off. You showed absolutely no emotions. How did you turn them off?"

"I turned off all my emotions many, many years ago. The violence, the mental and emotional abuse, and all the rest made me a living statue. I had no feelings of any kind. I didn't dare. Only recently have I begun to experience emotions I didn't know I had and to find a new life with Ron."

John ground his teeth and went over to give her a hug.

"If I ever see that Lane son of a bitch, I'll kill him!"

Sarah knew that Gentle John, for all his tough Marine Corps exterior, would never kill anyone away from the battlefield, but she was deeply touched by his reaction and Barbara's.

"I'll never forget that moment. It was tender, caring, and respectful. After nearly four decades of living, I was finally discovering what friendship really meant. Whenever I am alone, I tell myself my life is finally on a steady, even course. And I ask myself: Am I cured? My lips want to say 'Yes,' but my conscience is still saying 'Maybe.'

"Therapy, good friends, skilled doctors, and gentle Ron have changed the course of my life, but a nagging past returns to haunt me, though not so often as before. I lay my head on the pillow each night almost afraid to close my eyes and drift off, because I never know when the nightmare will repeat itself. In the nightmare, I am once again cornered by Lane and can't get away from him. Even though I haven't seen him in more than half a dozen years, he hovers over me."

Each time, he is faceless. She can identify him from the back, but she cannot make out his facial features. She didn't know the color of his eyes, because he always wore dark glasses, indoors and out. She can describe how he walks and how he holds his hands. He would always walk with his fists closed and clenched, as if he were constantly ready to hit someone, usually Sarah. Although she couldn't see his face in the nightmare, she could clearly make out his Fu Manchu mustache, which Sarah believed he wore to cover a scar received in a barroom battle.

But most menacing of all in the nightmare were those clenched hands, which he wielded like a weapon. They were the biographical index of the man himself. He once hired a writer to prepare a workbook to be used in his financial-management practice. The writer suggested instead that a book on Lane's life and experience as a planner might be more appropriate and might even become a national best-seller, if Lane would tell all. Reluctantly, Lane agreed. But in the course of the first interview, Sarah could see Lane pick constantly at his hands, and so could the writer. Lane had a chronic skin problem and would always pick away at scabs when he was nervous. It was as if the diseased hands revealed the crumbling character of the man in the body. He scrapped the biography idea in short order.

In Sarah's nightmare, the face of the monster is blank except for the mustache, but the sight of one hand picking constantly at the other is clear and unmistakable, because they are the hands that come at her and jar her awake with a scream.

"I believe strongly that God has put me in this position so that I may be a channel for helping others. It doesn't mean that I must now go out into the world and say that I have gone through Purgatory and I am now perfect. On the contrary. It is because I am not perfect and never will be that I must tell anyone who will listen that I am still learning. And would they like to learn along with me?

"At least I am comforted by the thought that my soul is no longer for sale to anyone. In the next 40 years, I hope I can banish that nightmare for good and find solace in lighting the way for other lost souls."

Sarah has no idea where Lane is, doesn't care, and doesn't want to know. Despite his violent behavior toward her, she would draw no comfort at all in seeing him humbled and jailed or whatever the law might prescribe. He is but one of many tyrants out there who treat women as dispensable toys and destroy their lives. She is far more interested in opening the eyes of all women and all decent men so that they will join forces against the Lanes of this world and the men—and women—who abuse or harass others.

In one of her sessions with John and Barbara, John asked: "Whatever happened to Mort the Assassin? Do you believe Lane invented the idea that he was a hit man and that he could hire Mort to execute anyone Lane wanted eliminated?"

Sarah smiled broadly: "As I look back on it today, I think it was all bluster on Lane's part and that Mort was only a gun dealer, who would never agree to kill anyone on contract. I can say that now."

"Why?"

"Because I am no longer afraid of dying."

About the Author

Lou (Louis R.) Guzzo has crowded several careers into one lifetime. His varied interests and accomplishments suggest he is something of a Renaissance man. He is the author, co-author, ghostwriter, and editor of 17 books, most of them related to the headliners he met as a newsman, a managing editor, a music, theater, films, and arts critic, a Governor's chief aide, and a TV and Radio commentator and editorial consultant.

A native of Cleveland, Ohio, his earliest interests were in music and theater. He is a violinist and pianist and, in his late teens, led his own dance orchestra. At the same time, he tried his hand at music composition, arranging for orchestra and chamber groups, and performing in amateur theater groups. For a time, he performed as a puppeteer for children's shows at Cleveland's Alta House.

However, it was journalism that attracted him when he found he could not make a living in music. How times have changed! He had shown favoritism for journalism at an early age. Lou was a columnist and editor of his high school newspaper, sports editor of his college newspaper (Case Western Reserve University), editor of the college's humor magazine, and, finally, editor of the university's newspaper.

Immediately upon graduation, the Second World War drastically changed the course of his life. After four and a half years of
service with the U.S. Army, Lou heeded the call of Horace Greeley
and moved to the West Coast with his new bride, Madeleine. The
Seattle Times hired him and soon discovered his wide experience in
music and all the arts. He was given the job of music, drama, films,
and arts critic, and within a short period became the most widely
read daily columnist in the region.

Lou broadened the critics' scope as few others have. He converted
his job into an "esthetic beat" as he began covering architectural,
environmental, archeological, beautification, and urban-planning
issues and meetings because he insisted they were all related to the
arts.

His remarkably broad interests led to his appointment in 1965 as
managing editor of the rival Seattle Post-Intelligencer. He may
have been the only music critic in American journalism to have
ascended to the powerful position of managing editor of a major
daily. Now he demonstrated a new bent; he became a crusading
editor, leading his staff to the investigation and eradication of a
county-wide bribery system involving officials at all levels. More
than 45 police officials, a chief of police, the county sheriff, the
county prosecutor, and two councilmen were indicted for playing
roles in the corrupt bribery and "tolerance policy" system.

Among his many other investigative pursuits, Lou turned the
newspaper into an extremely strong voice for women's rights and
an end to women's subservience to men. This book, "A Soul
Reclaimed," is a direct product of that campaign.

Upon retiring from the newspaper, Lou tried his hand in "the
other Washington," serving first as communications consultant to
the U.S. Atomic Energy Commission, then as a public-affairs officer in the State Department's Bureau of Oceans, International
Environmental and Scientific Affairs. He left to help run the

campaign of his longtime friend, Dr. Dixy Lee Ray, for Governor of Washington State. She won, and he became her chief policy adviser. He was also her education consultant, her director of cultural affairs, and the state historic preservation officer.

One more job remained, and it was ideal for a man with his wide experience. He served as daily commentator for KIRO-TV and Radio for a dozen years before retiring in 1995. Needless to say, he has spent most of his retirement time writing and speaking on the national lecture tour.